Wardens In Shackles

H. S. PABLA

By the author of
**Wildlife Conservation in India – 1
Road To Nowhere.**

2019

First Edition

Publisher: H. S. Pabla

Printed by: Kindle Direct Publishing

Cover Design by: Marco Moura (UK)

Available from amazon and other retail outlets

(E-book also available from Amazon channels)

Contents

List of Tables

List of Figures

List of Abbreviations

ADG	Additional Director General
AP	Andhra Pradesh
APCCF	Additional Principal Chief Conservator Of Forests
CEC	Central Empowered Committee
CM	Chief Minister
CWHs	Critical Wildlife Habitats
CWLW	Chief Wild Life Warden
DPR	Detailed Project Report
DWP	Director Of Wildlife Preservation
FDs	Forest Departments
FRA	Forest Rights Act, 2006 (The Scheduled Tribes and Other Trditional Forest Dwellers (Recognition of Forest Rights) Act, 2006)
GMAs	Game Management Areas
GoI	Government Of India
HWLW	Honorary Wildlife Warden
IAF	Indian Air Force
IFA 1927	Indian Forest Act 1927
IFS	Indian Forest Service
IUCN	International Union For Conservation Of Nature And Natural Resources
MFP	Minor Forest Produce (same as NTFP)
MoEF&CC	Ministry Of Environment Forests And Climate Change (new name of MoEF)
MP	Madhya Pradesh
NGO	Non-Governmental Organisation
NTCA	National Tiger Conservation Authority
PA	Protected Area
PCCF	Principal Chief Conservator Of Forests
PHVA	Habitat Viability Analysis
PIL	Public Interest Litigation
PTR	Panna Tiger Reserve

RF	Reserved Forest
SIT	Special Investigation Team
TCP	Tiger Conservation Plan
TR	Tiger Reserve
U.P.	Uttar Pradesh
WCS	Wildlife Conservation Society
WLPA	Wild Life Protection Act, 1972
WLS	Wildlife Sanctuary
WPSI	Wildlife Protection Society Of India
WTI	Wildlife Trust Of India

Acknowledgements

This book would not have been possible without the learning opportunities created by the Forest Department of Madhya Pradesh. I am grateful to everyone in this organisation who has ever been a part of my team or a facilitator. I do not want to name anyone because the contribution of those who may remain unnamed was no less.

I am deeply indebted to my wife, Harmohinder, who has always borne the burden of running our home alone and has had to endure endless days and nights worrying why I am rarely home despite being bodily there.

This book is dedicated to my parents and grandparents.

Preface

Conservation of wildlife is an endeavour to prevent extinctions and one of the methods is to reverse local extinctions before they grow to be global. We had lost the tiger from Panna, the gaur from Bandhavgarh, the blackbuck from Kanha, the great Indian bustard from Karera wildlife sanctuary during my lifetime, and more were on their way out, here and there. Except for the tigers of Panna, nobody had ever thought of bringing these species back. The question was whether we continue to count these extinctions and do nothing, or do something to reverse them while we still could. The answer was obvious but we had never learned to do it.

Once we had an idea how to build our capacity to reverse local extinctions, by associating with people who had moved thousands of animals across countries and continents, my struggle with Central institutions began. No one ever said what we wanted to do was wrong or unnecessary; they would just not let us do it.

As long as I was a field officer I never thought there was a problem with our systems, as the law gave me adequate powers to deal with wildlife crime, which is the primary job of a field officer. But when I came into supposedly decision-making positions, and wanted to do something more than just catching poachers, I started feeling stifled. Almost all my requests for mandatory permissions to do new things were either denied, or permissions were loaded with impossible conditions, or the permissions were withdrawn mid-course. Quite often, I had to find chinks in the law to do things which the law should have mandated.

I was director of Bandhavgarh National Park when I met the legendary teacher Allan Rodgers, perhaps for the first time, in 1986. After showing the park's management to his class for two-three days, he asked me "Why don't you start writing about wildlife management?" Although flattered, I told him that I knew nothing which others did not. For me, writing that I saw a tiger here and a gaur there did not seem like new knowledge. However, as time passed, I started feeling that I thought differently about wildlife matters and became quite vocal about the need to change our approach to conservation. It took me quite a while to figure out that wild animals and local people were living *off* each other and that the only way to conserve wildlife was to make them live *for* each other. Until I discovered this formula, I, like everyone else, had also lived by the unconvincing cliché that tigers and other big game needed to be saved for maintaining a healthy ecology in the country. However, I used to wonder if men could manage deer populations and our cows and machines could manage vegetation in our wilds, why we needed tigers, deer and elephants, especially when they would always be a threat to human life and property. Therefore, the justification for preserving such deadly animals had to be different from the one applicable to birds, butterflies and other small, even invisible organisms, without whom life on earth would just crash. Only religious and moral reasons were not enough to save them as they have to be killed when it becomes a matter of life and death for someone, and if dead animals were more valuable than alive. Therefore I started thinking taht we should have management systems aimed at generating clear cut economic benefits from these animals in order to earn them human care and sympathy beyond platitudes. When it finally dawned on me, my whole perspective on how conservation needed to be done changed. But, when I tried doing things which I had started advocating, such as using tourism as a conservation tool, treating wildlife as a natural resource, reversing local extinctions, etc. I discovered that I could not do anything worthwhile unless many more individuals and institutions thought like me. But, they did not. Then I started feeling that the country had started going the wrong way when the traditional emphasis on protected areas (PAs) started being replaced with the new-found love for wildlife corridors and landscapes, and when the Tribals and Other Forest Dwellers (Forest Rights) Act, 2006, popularly called the "Forest Rights Act, 2006" (FRA) was unleashed to dismantle everything that had been achieved in five decades of conservation. Why everybody did not think like me shall always remain a puzzle for me although we had the same concerns, and the solutions to most of our problems were obvious, if not easy. The only way to make the world think like me was to share my views with others, and hope that they would be embraced. As I am not a compulsive writer or speaker, the only way to do so was to write a book. However, when I started writing for the book, there was so much to say that it became too much, and too disparate, for a single book. Therefore, I decided to publish my thoughts in stages. That's how my first book, **"Wildlife Conservation in India - 1: Road To Nowhere"** was born. It explains the dilemma of preserving dangerous animals at the cost of forest dwellers in a poor country and advocates a win win approach, based on a symbiosis between men and wildlife.

When it came to preparing a sequel, the obvious choice was to tell the inside stories of how many of my ground breaking conservation projects were opposed by the agencies which were mandated to support my kind of work. For a long time I was tempted to name it as 'Conservation of Wildlife in India -2: Battles Within'. But then I realised that talking of my own struggles was not the purpose of the book. The real purpose was to illustrate that the states were powerless to discharge their conservation responsibilities because they have to take orders from the Centre on every small issue and that this was seriously hampering conservation. Most often the Centre becomes a hindrance in conservation rather than facilitating it. For example, the reintroduction of gaur (*Bos gaurus*) in Bandhavgarh National Park took five years from conception to action simply, because Delhi continued to block action for absolutely no reason. The states cannot decide on their own what needs to be done in conservation and have to follow Central guidelines which are often drafted by a person who has no or a very vague idea about the states other than his own. States are always evaluated on the basis of how diligently they comply with these guidelines, or advisories, rather than for any creative action. Interesting thing is that the States do not even protest against their neutering by the Central laws and meekly keep following the Central diktats. They seem to have lost all sense of ownership of their protected areas and wildlife and have become so accustomed to soliciting Central guidelines for everything that they have also lost all sense of creativity in conservation. Most often it looks the states are maintaining their natural resources not for themselves but for pleasing the Centre and keep looking over their shoulders to know what the Centre thinks of their performance.

The stories in this book highlight the shackles which the states, the wardens of wildlife on the ground, have to carry while trying to preserve our natural heritage. Therefore, I decided to rename the book as **"Wildlife Conservation in India - 2: Wardens in Shackles"**.

Although the book details several projects representing conservation success in India, these projects happened despite the Central agencies' opposition, rather than because of them. Apart from the successful projects, the book also contains a brief description of several still-born projects which could not see the light of the day because the complicated decision making processes in the country rarely let anything of significance happen (see 'Unfinished Dreams'). Although all of these projects were not killed by the Central agencies, many of them did not reach the Centre because the state authorities were apprehensive of the opposition of the Centre.

Although the drama in these stories should make some exciting reading in itself, they are more important for illustrating the imbalance of power between the centre and the states, and the damage it is doing to conservation of wildlife in the country.

"**Wardens In Shackles**" is an anguished cry of a Chief Wild Life Warden (CWLW) to unshackle his office to enable him to do his job, i.e. preserve wildlife of the State. The book describes the cavalier manner in which the GoI and its agencies treat the states in conservation matters, and shows that without dogged pursuit, and some madness on someone's part, nothing worthwhile can be done in the field of conservation. That our initiatives succeeded is almost a miracle, as only some extraordinary coincidences made these successes possible. Perhaps Shahrukh Khan was right when he said, "*agar kisi cheez ko dil se chaho ... to puri kainaat use tumse milane ki koshish mein lag jaati hai*" (if you want something from the heart, all the forces of nature start working to get it for you). There is no other explanation for Jairam Ramesh (the minister), P.B. Gangopadhyay (CWLW MP), and Les Carlisle (from South Africa) coming together just to fulfil my dream of restoring locally extinct species to some of our prized parks! While the world already knows the scientific and technical aspects of these operations from the research papers and technical reports already published, nobody, except me, knows how much pain and hard work went into getting the go-ahead for them. These stories need to be told in the hope that they may trigger a review of the way we do things in government.

The most important message of the book is that conservation decision making in India is messy and we need to review our systems with the objective of empowering the states to do what they think best for *their* wildlife. Investing absolute powers in the Central agencies regarding field level matters is a recipe for inefficiency and it stifles creativity in the states. The prevailing narrative in Delhi that the states will destroy everything if left to themselves is unacceptable and fallacious. It is the states, not the Centre, who created all the PAs in the country. How can they dismantle them? As I have said elsewhere, if the states make mistakes, the damage will be local; but, if GoI makes a mistake it will affect the entire country. We must learn a lesson from the case of wildlife tourism which narrowly escaped being outlawed as a result of too much power being vested in NTCA. Similarly, heavens would not have fallen, if GoI had allowed the reintroduction of tiger in Madhav National Park or reintroduction of white tiger in Sanjay Tiger Reserve, the park from where the last wild white tiger was captured.

We all know that government systems are not made for efficiency, but not many know that they actually end up killing creativity and innovation. One of the worst examples is the Wild Life (Protection) Act, 1972 (WLPA). Every intervention under this law is required to be approved by so many authorities and boards that by the time a decision is made the protagonist is either transferred or he/she retires. The next man either does not have his heart in it or may be just reluctant to take the risk of failure. The approving authorities may not all agree with each other, or some may be just reluctant to take responsibility. And, in most cases, if it is not my idea, it is a useless idea.

The book also illustrates how it is still possible to repair some of the damage that has already been done to our wildlife. The country needs to come out of the passive conservation mode, focused just on preventing future damage, and should start restocking depleted areas through translocation of prey and predators. Madhya Pradesh now has the capacity to undertake mass translocation of wild animals either to create new wildlife reserves or to decongest existing ones or to reinforce dwindling populations. Other states can learn and adapt these techniques to suit their requirements.

Lastly, I wish to mention that this book is not meant to undermine any institutions or disparage any persons. Nor it is meant to be an autobiography. The institutions, persons and my own self find mention only because they are central to the events which I want to share with the readers. I am painfully conscious of the fact that some of my comments about these institutions, and the persons running them, may not be very charitable to them, but I just could not find any other way of describing those events. I have tried my best to be as objective in describing these events as possible. But I hope the reader will forgive me if at places I give the impression of being emotional and one-sided, as it is tough to be entirely objective when you yourself are a central character in the drama.

CHAPTER 1

Introduction

Wildlife conservation in India is governed by the Wild Life (Protection) Act, 1972 (WLPA). Apart from defining offences and penalties, the original Act only provided for the creation of protected areas (PAs) and regulation of hunting and trade in wildlife. States were fully empowered to do whatever they thought was good for their wildlife and wildlife habitats. 'Forests and Wildlife' was still a state subject and the Centre could make any laws on this subject only if more than half the states requested the Centre to do so. The power of Mrs. Indira Gandhi was at its peak and most of the states were ruled by her party. Although the law did not encroach upon any of the states' rights, she still had to personally intervene with some states to get their consent for making a Central law for the conservation of wildlife (Ranjitsinh 2017). Since then the law has been amended many times primarily to transfer the powers of the states to the Central government or its statutory authorities. The law, as it stands today, gives the states virtually no role of any significance in decision making related to wildlife conservation. The only power left with the state was under section 29, basically to remove any wildlife or forest produce from a wildlife sanctuary (WLS), "for the better management of wildlife". Even this has now been snatched by the Supreme Court saying that *"we restrain respondents ... from ordering the removal of dead, diseased, dying or wind-fallen tree, drift wood and grasses, etc. from any National Park or Game Sanctuary or forest."* (Order dated 14.02.2000 in IA no. 548 in WP 202/1995). So, now the states have to get the approval of the Central Government and its statutory authorities and boards for doing anything even slightly different from routine protection, and have to follow their directions and advisories. Although the constitution requires that the Centre cannot make any laws on an item in the concurrent list without consulting the states, I am sure they did not consult the states when the law was amended in 2006, making the most far-reaching changes to date. Although we objected to several provisions inserted in the Act in 2006, this was only when the law had already been passed. I do not think our complaints went beyond the table of some lowly clerk in GoI or the NTCA which had already occupied conservation centre-stage by then.

When the WLPA was promulgated in 1972, there were only two statutory authorities, namely the Director of Wildlife Preservation (DWP) in Delhi and the Chief Wild Life Wardens

(CWLWs) in states. CWLW was virtually the CEO of conservation in the state and had nearly absolute authority for running the show. Since then several new authorities and boards have been created, under the WLPA, who issue directions to State Governments and CWLWs on the silliest of matters, virtually on a day-to-day basis. NTCA is the most powerful authority on wildlife conservation in the country now, and has the mandate not only to deal with tiger conservation, but also on all other conservation matters as provided under section 38–O of the Act, quoted below:

"**Powers and Functions of Tiger Conservation Authority.**—The Tiger Conservation Authority shall have the following powers and perform the following functions, namely:—

(a) *to approve the Tiger Conservation Plan prepared by the State Government under sub-section (3) of section 38V of this Act;*

(b) *evaluate and assess various aspects of sustainable ecology and disallow any ecologically unsustainable land use such as, mining, industry and other projects within the tiger reserves;*

(c) *lay down normative standards for tourism activities and guidelines for project tiger from time to time for tiger conservation in the buffer and core area of tiger reserves and ensure their due compliance;*

(d) *provide for management focus and measures for addressing conflicts of men* and wild animal and to emphasize on co-existence in forest areas outside the National Parks, sanctuaries or tiger reserve, in the working plan code;

(e) provide information on protection measures including future conservation plan, estimation of population of tiger and its natural prey species, status of habitats, disease surveillance, mortality survey, patrolling, reports on untoward happenings and such other management aspects as it may deem fit including future plan conservation;

(f) approve, co-ordinate research and monitoring on tiger, co-predators, prey, habitat, related ecological and socio-economic parameters and their evaluation;

(g) ensure that the tiger reserves and areas linking one protected area or tiger reserve with another protected area or tiger reserve are not diverted for ecologically unsustainable uses, except in public interest and with the approval of the National Board for Wild Life and on the advice of the Tiger Conservation Authority;

(h) facilitate and support the tiger reserve management in the State for biodiversity conservation initiatives through eco-development and people's participation as per approved management plans and to support similar initiatives in adjoining *areas consistent with the Central and State laws;*

(i) ensure critical support including scientific, information technology and legal support for better implementation of the tiger conservation plan;

(j) facilitate ongoing capacity building programme for skill development of officers and staff of tiger reserves; and

(k) perform such other functions as may be necessary to carry out the purposes of this Act with regard to conservation of tigers and their habitat.

2. The Tiger Conservation Authority may, in the exercise of its powers and performance of its functions under this Chapter, issue directions in writing to any person, officer or authority for the protection of tigers or tiger reserves and such person, officer or authority shall be bound to comply with the directions: Provided that no such direction shall interfere with or affect the rights of local people particularly the Scheduled Tribes".

A special note needs to be taken of clause (g) above, which brings virtually the entire country under the control of NTCA. Sub-section (2) is unique, perhaps in the whole world, as no authority, except the courts, is ever given a power which every *"person, officer or authority"* is *"bound to comply with"* anywhere. This means non-compliance is a punishable offence!

As mentioned under (a) above, NTCA has been given the mandate to approve the Tiger Conservation Plan (TCP) of every tiger reserve (TR). The TCP is not an ordinary document carrying a list of mundane things to be done in a TR. The TCP can cover unlimited area outside the boundaries of the TR, both forest as well non-forest, to ensure *"ecologically compatible land uses in ... areas linking one protected area or tiger reserve with another"* and *"forestry operations of regular forest divisions ... are not incompatible with the needs of tiger conservation"* (section 38V). As I often jokingly say, one would need the permission of the NTCA if one wants to build a house in the middle of Delhi, as PAs are all over the country. And building a house anywhere is in no way an "ecologically compatible" land use!

Further, in view of NTCA's mandate to ensure *"ecologically compatible land uses in ... areas linking one protected area or tiger reserve with another"*, strengthened by some utterances of the Supreme Court of India, all development projects *anywhere* in India now have also to be cleared by NTCA besides the CWLW, State Board for Wild Life (SBWL), State Government, National Board for Wild Life (NBWL) and MoEF&CC. The number of these projects is so large and the political pressure to clear them is so severe that these bodies do virtually nothing but clear these projects. Although the boards now meet very regularly, primarily to clear these projects, still the country is unhappy with the obstructions that the wildlife clearances, along with other environmental laws, create in the economic development of the country. So much so that the government once constituted a committee, under the chairmanship of a former cabinet secretary, to review all environmental laws in order to reduce the nuisance of forestry and wildlife clearances. Although nothing much came out of the recommendations of this committee, this shows that even the Central Government, which made these laws, is fed up with them.

One might ask why I am worried about the strengthening of the wildlife Act. There are two reasons for this. Firstly, all the amenments of the law are taking away the powers of the States to conserve their wildlife as per their vision. That also means taking away the powers of the CWLW, the chair in which I felt helpless to do what I thought was right. Secondly, I am worried about the backlash from the society if conservation concerns become too much of a hassle for the country. The stirrings are already there, as indicated by the constitution of the committee mentioned above. Next time the country may actually act on the recommendations of such a committee, taking the country back to where it all began, 50 years ago, when nobody cared about wildlife and nature.

So it is in such an environment that the states have to conserve their wildlife, through their CWLWs who have virtually no power to do or decide anything on their own. Therefore, nobody on the ground ever thinks of anything new in conservation as all initiative is arrogated by the Centre to itself. If ever someone dares to dream, these initiatives would often go nowhere as the Central approval, if ever given, will come with arbitrary, impossible conditions, after so much delay, that either the project becomes irrelevant or impossible to implement by then.

As shown in the following pages, every single one of our path-breaking conservation initiatives suffered almost insurmountable obstructions from GoI and went through only because I, as the CWLW of MP, refused to quit.

Until 2006, the Centre-state relations on wildlife conservation were virtually limited to the Centre providing funds to the states under certain centrally sponsored schemes, such as Project Tiger and Development of National Parks and Sanctuaries (now called Integrated Development of Wildlife Habitats), and all the Central directives to the states were related to the implementation of these schemes. Since the creation of the NTCA in 2006, the relationship between the Centre and the states has undergone a qualitative change and has virtually turned into a superior-subordinate equation. NTCA is now bigger than the DWP, in terms of both clout and budget, and calls all the shots as every *"person, officer or authority shall be bound to comply with the directions"* of the NTCA.

This situation may be all right for those CWLWs who do not have a mind of their own and pass their days in this chair just as in any other routine posting. But if some CWLW has a vision and wants to do something more than the routine stuff, he has to pander to the whims and fancies of the mandarins running the Central bodies, besides taking the State along. Often, Central bodies issue directives which the states do not agree with or find difficult to implement but comply with them without demur. NTCA's stand on wildlife tourism is a glaring example of how the Central bodies ride roughshod over the states. As discussed in the chapter entitled 'Saving Wildlife Tourism', NTCA started issuing directives to the states to "phase out" tourism from PAs in 2006 which the states did not agree with. But none of the states, except MP, objected to them. Perhaps the states have become completely used to these fetters and start feeling uncomfortable without them.

These fetters need to be removed if we want our natural heritage conserved. Why should simple operations like capture of an animal or managing tourism in PAs need any Central permission or interference? The attitude of the Central officials, particularly those in NTCA, to the proposals for the reintroduction of tiger, gaur, blackbuck, *barasinghas* and white tiger into their former habitats was utterly unsupportive. These were novel projects, which, apart from restoring local biodiversity, were aimed at building the capacity of the State in active wildlife management, i.e. capture and translocation of large mammals. But GoI placed as many roadblocks in our path as possible. Although all these projects were ultimately executed almost flawlessly, heavens would not have fallen if there had been some mistakes or failures.

Unless we encourage our field officers to try new techniques, even if they make some mistakes, how will the country move forward? Every country has gone through its own learning curve in developing wildlife management techniques as per the needs of its unique fauna. South Africa started with 50% mortality in translocation and was able to bring it down to 2%, through experimentation and innovation (Les Carlisle, pers. comm.). Without creating an environment for innovation and creativity, by simplifying the procedures and permissions, India is never going to be able to do it, and we will perhaps remain content to be good in counting extinctions. For India to succeed in conservation, the primary requirement is to dismantle the authoritarian institutions like NTCA and create new ones with the mandate for adopting and adapting global wildlife management practices, rather than undermining the ownership, initiative and motivation of the states.

It is nobody's case that the States should be completely independent of the Central policies. The need is to modernise wildlife conservation in India and give States adequate space to experiment with different approaches based on their special socio-economic and ecological realities. While the Centre may decide what to support and what not, based on its own policies, which must also be crafted in consultation with the states, it should have no veto power on State programmes. The logic of its advisories and its financial support should be the only means of influencing state programmes. Main role of the Centre in conservation matters must be to financially and technically support what it thinks is the right approach to conservation and creating capacity building institutions.

The chapter entitled as "The Panna Story" takes a fresh and comprehensive look at the extinction of tigers from Panna Tiger Reserve, with the considerable advantage of hindsight. Four chapters highlight the events which made the reintroduction of tigers, gaur, blackbuck and barasingha into their former ranges so difficult mainly because the Central authorities placed every possible roadblock in their path. The chapter entitled as "Saving Wildlife Tourism" discusses the sustained efforts of NTCA to outlaw tourism in tiger reserves and how it was forced to change its stand in the Supreme Court under public pressure. The final chapter entitled as "The Unfinished Dreams" lists a series of projects which could never see the light of the day because of our complex decision making processes but which could have created, potentially, a totally new roadmap for conservation of wildlife in India.

This book is neither an armchair criticism of the government by an outsider nor the recriminations of a failed bureaucrat. This is a call for making our great successes in conservation of iconic wildlife look ordinary by creating an environment that encourages innovation and accountability and, thereby, leads to even more remarkable achievements.

CHAPTER 2

The Panna Tiger Extinction

Of all the places where I have worked, I have had the longest, and the strongest, association with Panna National Park. This love affair started much before the loss and subsequent redemption of Panna's tigers, and still continues in some ways. I was its first director, between 1982 and 1986, I set up its first administration, and, it was here that I earned my spurs as a young wildlifer. Although already a sanctuary since 1975, I found most of it a desolate wasteland run over by thousands of heads of cattle and buffalos from nearly 50 local villages and several cattle camps, and alarming levels of illicit felling of teak (*Tectona grandis*). However, the records also showed the presence of some 15 tigers. This was in stark contrast to lush green Kanha where, during my short stint, managing tourism and VIPs seemed to be the core concern. We were able to banish nearly 80,000 heads of livestock from the park, in the first monsoon itself, moved out two villages, Khairayya and Khamaria, significantly stemmed rampant illicit felling, and had reasonably disciplined the actions and movements of the people in the park before I moved on to Bandhavgarh (Pabla 1984). It was quite gratifying when, years later, people gave me some of the credit for the making of this tiger reserve. However, all the bouquets turned into bags of brickbats, the moment the report of the Special Investigation Team (SIT) was out in 2009, when I was made out to be the principal accused for the extinction of tigers from the park (Sen et al. 2009). Although the tigers are back in Panna, and we have already given the world some new science and understanding about conservation, the media, spurred on by some self-appointed angels of conservation, continued to harp on the need to punish the *guilty* for a long time, rather than focusing on the tremendous scientific, management and administrative lessons that this case has thrown up. The story of this extinction is known to the world only through the media clamour for 'whodunnit?' while the real story is much more complex and instructive. Here is the tale that will ensure that the tigers, or any other species, will never go extinct now, if we remember these lessons, even casually.

The rise and fall of tigers in Panna

The routine estimations carried out in the Gangou wildlife sanctuary, which largely comprises the present Panna National Park, reported approximately 15-16 tigers before 1982. However, when we made our first assessment in the winter of 1984, the number came to be 23, including cubs of all ages (Pabla 1984). People might repudiate these pugmark-based figures, as seems to be the fashion today, but we were quite confident of the veracity of these figures. We had no tourism back then, but seeing tigers or tiger signs was a regular affair for the staff and the rare visitors we got. Once Dr. Ranjitsinh and late Mr. Peter Jackson, the venerable Chairman of the Cat Specialist Group of IUCN, saw the pugmarks of tigers on seven different roads in a single morning. Some places like Balayya Seha and Huddi were almost synonymous with tigers. I, along with a few friends, once saw a family of six tigers, of which four must have been nearly adult cubs, at Balayya Seha. Chand Khan, the mahout who was detailed to record tiger presence at Balayya Seha every day, before we bought elephants, recorded tiger sightings on 84% of the days he was there, including some interesting stories of bears chasing tigers out of the caves. With some possible exceptions, the park continued to be managed by very able officers right up to the turn of the century, when Dr. Raghunandan Singh Chundawat (Raghu for everyone) started talking of mismanagement and rampant poaching.

Raghu and Panna

Raghu and I were colleagues in the Wildlife Institute of India (WII). After completing his Ph.D. on snow leopards, he wanted to work with tigers and requested my help in locating a 'sub-optimal' tiger habitat for his research in MP. We travelled to Kanha, Bandhavgarh and Panna together, perhaps in November 1994, to look at potential sites, and he plumped for Panna the moment he saw it. I will always remember the magic of the full-moon night we spent on the roof of the abandoned school building, in Badgadi, which is now converted into a sort of a rest house, surrounded by a sea of grass unleashed by the relocation of the village. When Raghu started his research in 1995, he found only a small tiger population numbering approximately 10-15, which grew to 29 by 2002, (Karanth et. al. 2004) even by his own estimates, although the precision of his estimate was quite low, compared with later estimates by WII. This was about the time when Raghu started alerting the world that tiger numbers in the park were declining under severe poaching pressure, so that when, in 2005, the forest department came up with the figure of 34-35 tigers in the park, he vehemently rubbished it. When in 2006, the WII estimated the tiger population to be 15-32 in the entire Panna landscape of nearly 787 km^2 (Jhala *et. al.* 2008), which was not much different from his own estimate, in view of the better precision of the former, he continued to question these figures. Although the WII report, which labelled the condition of Panna's tiger population as 'healthy' in the context of the overall situation in the country, comforted the department to some extent that the state of affairs was not as bad as made out by Raghu, it neither lulled the government into sleep, nor did it douse the media fires stoked by Raghu's persistent flaying of the park management.

Poaching is a fact of life and can never be totally eliminated. Panna was no different. Poaching had been consistently recorded in Panna also, ever since my time, or since Raghu had started his work in Panna. One tiger had got snared in village Harsa, just outside the park in 1985 and some of Raghu's collared tigers were either poisoned or snared. Although only one tiger death had been actually recorded in the park between 2000 and 2005, it is interesting to analyse why Raghu suddenly became rather hostile to the park management by the year 2000 and started making a big noise about alleged poaching in the park. Until then, everything wrong with the park was not attributed to bad management, though every tiger death was bemoaned. Later on, he virtually started running a campaign against the park management, and still later, against the forest department itself. Irrespective of the fact whether Raghu was right or wrong, there is a more human element to the story.

When Raghu came to Panna in 1995, he was immediately treated like a member of the family and was given full freedom to work. He was even allowed to build a house inside the park, and was allowed free access to the departmental elephants and in every way he was made to feel as a part of the forest department. To some extent, this was, perhaps, because of his association with me. To his credit, Raghu provided some novelty and technical content to park management, which was plain and simple patrolling and protection till then, in the form of radio telemetry, transect counts, bird counts etc. Until early 2000, Mr. P.K. Chaudhary was the Field Director and Raghu had a good equation with him. In 2000, Mr. S.K.S. Chauhan replaced Mr. Chaudhary, for a few months, before he was replaced by Mr. Sanjay Mukharia. Mr. Chauhan had been director of Bandhavgarh National Park in the early eighties and had started the *tiger show* there, for the first time. When he saw that his park had enough tigers and three elephants, he started tracking tigers for tourists, *a la* Kanha and Bandhavgarh. As the elephants got busier with tourism, Raghu started complaining about the non-availability of elephants for his research work. In 2001, when Mr. Mukharia and his deputy Mr. Vijay Ambade were posted there, things took a turn for the worse. By then, Raghu had severed his connection with WII, and was doing his research privately, with foreign funding, and was no longer seen as a part of the establishment as earlier, and, perhaps, evoked some jealousy among the park staff due to the attention he was getting. The BBC made a documentary, called 'The Emerald Forest', on the park, in which it appeared as if Raghu was running the park and the tigers were doing well primarily because of his research. This also created some heartburns among the senior staff. As a result of the decline in mutual trust, things started to deteriorate by the day. Raghu's suggestions regarding park management, which were taken seriously by the earlier managers, started being ignored and spurned, and he was asked to limit his role to his research. Miffed at this treatment, Raghu started writing letters to the park management, and their superiors, possibly less to improve park management and more to create a record against the field director and the deputy director. Perhaps in retaliation, the management started tightening the screws on Raghu. The availability of elephants to Raghu was further reduced as there was no commitment from the department to provide free elephants for his research. He was asked to record his and his assistants' movements in a register kept at the park gate. His access to the forests at night was also disallowed. He also started complaining to the higher-ups regarding alleged mismanagement in the park. The situation became so bad that the park management even seized his vehicle, once, for entering the park at night.

As long as the problem was between the park management and Raghu, the higher officers were trying to resolve the issues to the best of their capacity, although neither of the parties was satisfied with the results. He came to me with these issues a few times, although I was not responsible for the administration of the park. I did speak with the relevant people, but the relations continued to deteriorate. However, when he, through Belinda Wright of the Wildlife Protection Society of India (WPSI), filed a public interest litigation (PIL) in the Supreme Court, perhaps in 2003, in which even petty issues were included, the situation became completely intractable. Among the allegations included in the PIL, along with heavy poaching of wild animals, were issues like why a certain fire line was not exactly 15 feet wide as provided in the management plan, why stones dug out from a *nullah* were used in the construction of a temporary patrolling camp near Kharaiyya, why woody plants invading an important grassland (Bhadaar) were removed, why a patrolling camp was built in the middle of a grassland, why certain grasslands were burnt, and so on. Obviously, neither the court nor the Central Empowered Committee could have given any direction on these technical matters, as every action has both positive as well as negative implications and it is possible to justify most management actions depending upon the objectives one is working for. Even if Raghu did not agree with some of these actions, he could have lived with these so-called errors of judgment, but he chose to escalate the matters and destroyed his bridges with the department completely. My advice to him, all along, was that he should retain his acceptability with the department to be able to contribute to the cause which was so dear to him.

His usual refrain was that *he was not there to make friends while tigers were dying.*

The Central Empowered Committee (CEC) visited the park in the summer of 2004, along with the petitioner, Ms. Belinda Right and Mr. SC Sharma, former Additional DGF (Wildlife) in Government of India. Although I was not in the wildlife wing yet, the Principal Chief Conservator of Forests (PCCF) (Mr. AP Dwivedi) asked me to accompany him to Panna, perhaps in view of my good acquaintance with the park. At the end of the visit, the PCCF and the CEC (Mr. Jayakrishanan and Mr. Valmik Thapar) agreed on two immediate actions: One that Mr. Vijay Ambade, the deputy director with whom Raghu had particularly bad relations, should be transferred, and secondly, Raghu's permission for further research, which was due for renewal shortly, should be withheld, in view of the bitter relations between him and the park management. Expectedly, all the recommendations of the CEC were rejected by the department, except the one related to the demolition of the camp established in the middle of the Bhadaar grassland. The Chairman of the CEC made another surprise visit to the park, in May 2005, which resulted in the famous *'Panna is showing signs of Sariska'* comment and an immediate rebuttal by the state government, accusing the CEC of making such alarmist statements at the behest of a *'disgruntled scientist'*. Till then the government was confident that there was nothing seriously wrong with the park as the tiger census, conducted under the supervision of the staff from other parks, had reported 34 tigers in the park, which was later partially confirmed by the WII's assessment conducted in the later part of 2005/2006.

Raghu has been portrayed, by the media and the conservation world, as the wronged whistle-blower whose permission to continue research in the park was cancelled because he dared to blow the lid from the alleged mismanagement of the Panna Tiger Reserve. Although I have had my sympathies with Raghu, I think this charge is not correct. It would have been difficult for any government to allow the festering relations between the park management and the researcher to continue. The case for renewing his research permission was still pending when I moved into the office of the Chief Wildlife Warden, as APCCF, in June 2005. Despite my dilemma on the issue, I supported the decision of the CWLW to refuse permission since the permission would have been an invitation to further embarrassment for the government, as Raghu could have used his position to undermine the government's case in the court, apart from our having to deal with regular feuds between him and the park management. Apart from that, we reviewed all his reports before taking a decision, and agreed that the project, which had already run for more than ten years, was unlikely to produce any great new results. By then people had already started viewing his research as a vested interest for getting foreign funds to make a living. I think Raghu's presence in the park was very useful, if not for the research he did, then, as mentioned earlier, for providing some technical colour to park management, and for his following the tigers, day and night, which must have given them some added security. The profile of the park also went up as his research was a popular media subject and important people had started visiting the park to see his work. I think the state government recognized this fact and even made him a member of the State Board for Wildlife. But when it came to fighting a court battle, no holds were barred. When he started portraying all foresters as incompetent and ignorant, the state dug out all his land deals in the area, issued notice for recovering the dues for using government elephants for nearly ten years, and even registered an offence for filming with the BBC at night without permission.

While Raghu was claiming that there were very few tigers in the park, the 2005 census showed the presence of 34 tigers. When Raghu, and, at his behest, many others, branded this assessment as a cover up, the CWLW ordered a repeat census, under the supervision of Mr. Aseem Srivastava, Deputy Director of Kanha Tiger Reserve and invited all the doubting Thomases to participate in the exercise. This exercise produced 35 tigers but the exercise was immediately rejected by the critics. Both the exercises were based on the traditional 'pug mark' method. In its sincerity, the department requested WII to conduct another assessment. WII proposed to do it by analysing the digital images of plaster casts of tiger pugmarks, but abandoned the exercise in the middle saying that the sample size was not sufficient for this method. This, I can now recall, was the first inkling that, after all, Raghu might be right about the tiger population in the park. In the meantime, the process for the all-India assessment of 'Tigers and Co-Predators', using camera traps, had started, and we requested WII to produce an advance report for Panna, as the Supreme Court had also desired WII's views on the issue. WII gave its report in October 2006, estimating the tiger numbers in the Panna *landscape* to be 24 (range 15—32). Although this number was lower than the 34—35 animals reported by the department or 29 animals reported by Raghu a few years ago, the difference was explained in terms of the difference in technologies and precision levels. Although the tiger density in the park was certainly lower than what was claimed by the park management, it was, ostensibly, not as bad as claimed by Raghu, especially as WII termed the situation as 'healthy' in view of the all-India scenario.

Revamp of park management

I joined the wildlife wing in June 2005, at the peak of this numbers game. Despite the continuing stand-off between the department and the non-official conservationists, led by Raghu, a complete overhaul of the park administration was done. A new director and deputy director were posted and they were given a free hand to choose their team. To ensure that there should be no let up at least on the protection side, whatever resources were requested by the new director were provided. The new team was confident that tiger density in the park was adequate, more so after the results of WII's assessment came in. The decline in Panna from 29 or 35 tigers to 24 was commensurate with the overall decline in tiger numbers in the state, from 704 to 300, and could be reasonably explained in terms of general decline or the change of methodology, and nothing particularly alarming seemed to have happened in Panna. As a result, the concerns expressed by the activists and the media did not seem to be justified. But the department did not want to take any chances and did whatever seemed reasonable to rule out any chance of a further decline in tiger numbers that could be attributed to lack of security. The new director, Mr. Shahbaz Ahmed, who had a reputation of being a no-nonsense officer, initiated a very intensive monitoring programme, and constructed nearly 70 new observation posts (*nigrani chowkies*) at vantage points to keep a 24×7 vigil in the park. Raids on several suspected poachers were also launched including some on the basis of information provided by Raghu. One prize catch in these raids was the notorious pardhi Baraf Singh, whose name had appeared in the statement of Mohammad Rais of Chhatarpur captured by police. Senior officers regularly held meetings of police officers and district administration in Panna to emphasise the need for interdepartmental coordination in securing the park. Principal Secretary Forests, Mr. Avani Vaish himself took a meeting of forest, police and revenue officers to tone up the administration, in February 2008. Despite all these efforts, one tigress with two female cubs was poisoned in May 2006. The body of the second cub was never recovered.

Despite all the strengthening, and the comfort of the WII report that tiger presence in the park was 'healthy', the tiger sightings by visitors had come down significantly by 2007. Mr. Shyamendra Singh (Vini) who has been running a lodge in Panna since the eighties, and has a very good understanding of the natural history of the area, was very emphatic that tiger numbers in the park had come down, whatever the census reports may say. Raghu continued to emphasise the fact, whenever we met, that there were very few tigers in the park. While not arguing about the actual numbers, we used to ask everyone what they thought should be done to check any further decline, but no worthwhile suggestions came our way. The problem for us was that on one side we had the WII report which gave a reasonable number, on the other we had these reports. The park management also did not alert us of anything unusual, as they were doing what they thought was necessary for protection. When Shahbaz left in 2007, Mr. G Krishnamurthy came as the field director. While continuing with earlier systems of monitoring, patrolling, and 24×7 observation posts, he designated all the daily wages staff as *Bagh Rakshaks* (Protectors of Tigers) to keep them motivated, and started an intensive programme to educate the surrounding villages about the threats posed by professional poachers like *pardhis*. He prepared several sets of flip charts on what *pardhis* look like, what they do etc., exhorting locals to report the presence of *pardhis* anywhere near the park. He distributed them to various beats for interacting with nearby villagers. Mr. L.K. Chowdhary replaced Mr. G. Krishnamuthy in 2008 and started a system of patrolling the roads outside the park, in coordination with the neighbouring divisions, so that the security umbrella could be expanded. The process of relocation of villages, resurrected by Sanjay Mukharia after a 12-15 year hiatus, was continued and 11 more villages were relocated while this controversy was raging.

Tiger signs all over but no tigress

Towards the end of 2007, the park management noticed that, although tigers were there in the park, there were no females. No cubs had been seen in the park for almost five years, except the ones that had died with their mother in May 2006. It was clear that there were no *breeding* tigresses in the park, but the stark realization that there were no females *at all* was shocking. This meant that there were no chances of the revival of the population. I, along with Khageshwar Nayak, former field director of Kanha Tiger Reserve, rushed to Panna on the 19th of December 2007, to assess the situation. The presence of Mr. Nayak, who had had a long stint in Kanha, was meant to supplement my rather dated field experience with his relatively fresh field exposure, as I wanted to be absolutely sure of the situation. I requested the park management to preserve all the tiger signs they could detect in the park for our investigations. We stayed there till the 21st of December and went to almost every corner of the park east of the Ken, to investigate the tiger signs preserved by the staff. In the afternoon of the 19th, fresh pugmarks of a male tiger on the road in Panna Seha were seen. Next day, one tiger was seen at the tiger show in Hinouta range. I remember seeing fresh pugmarks near Nararan, again near Khamaria, a few-days-old kill in the Madla range, old pugmarks in a dry stream bed in Panna range, fresh pug marks in the Amdar area, and rather fresh tiger scats in the Panna range. When I reached my old favourite, Balayya *Seha*, I was surprised to hear that our people no longer waited for tigers there and no one remembered the pre-eminence of this spot in the tiger history of this park. When I left the spot, the local forest guard stayed back, perhaps to test the truth of my words. Within an hour or so, we got a wireless message that a tiger entered the *seha* (gorge) in full view of the forest guard and his assistant.

I remember talking to some of my old associates in the staff about the health of the park. They informed me that the park was infested with dacoit gangs, led by Mohan Patel, Dhaniram Patel and the infamous Thokia (*doctor* Ambika Patel), who had sworn vengeance against the park. The staff were scared and dared not investigate any gun shots heard in the park, especially at night. Although their impression was that the tiger numbers had gone down significantly, they could still mention some specific tigers visiting their areas. I think we saw tiger pug marks at 8-10 places in the two days we were in the park, apart from the actual sightings, kills and scats, but could not clearly agree whether any of these tracks were females. I mentally compared the incidence of tiger signs with my own days, and the intervening periods, and felt that seeing tiger signs in 8-10 places in a park, and physical encounters with two tigers, in two days, should be all that is expected in an average park. We did not discuss the numbers but were reasonably happy with what we had seen. Nayak agreed with me. Dr. Rajesh Gopal, Member Secretary of the NTCA, knew that I was in Panna and called me to know my findings on the morning of 20th December, and I assured him that the tiger presence seemed to be reasonably good in the park. On my return, I informed the government of my impressions. Although we could not confirm whether there were any tigresses in the park, we felt that if there were tigers in the park, some of them must be females. I thought the males would attract females, if there were any within a reasonable distance, sooner or later. However, that was not to be.

NTCA's fact finding team finds 7 tigers

While I thought NTCA would accept my word that the park still had tigers, another fact-finding team was sent by the Authority to Panna. This team, consisting of Mr. Ravi Singh, Secretary General of WWF India, and Mr. P.K. Sen, former director of Project Tiger, toured the park for two and a half days from the 8th to the 10th January 2008 and reported that they saw the signs of seven adult and 2-3 sub adult tigers and 'underlined' the excellent management of the park (Sen and Singh 2008). They had ignored all single pugmarks and had taken only long trails into account in their assessment.

Later, in 2009, when the park had lost all the tigers, and Mr. Sen returned to Panna as a member of the Special Investigation Team (SIT) to investigate the loss, he conveniently forgot his earlier findings while condemning the park management. Rather than admitting that their earlier findings may have been wrong, as it is not easy to assess the tiger numbers from a hasty examination of tracks and signs, rumours were spread that the tiger pugmarks seen by them, back in January 2008, may have been planted. Similar doubts were also spread about my own visit of December 2007. I was understandably troubled to hear such things but could not accept these allegations, for several reasons, despite having an open mind. First, Mr. Krishnamuthy had just joined as Field Director. Therefore, it would have been more convenient for him to say that he inherited few tigers rather than personally risking blame for the impending decline or for fudging the evidence. Secondly, it would have been impossible to do such a dastardly thing secretly, in the entire park, as it would have involved several people who would have been prone to spilling the beans, especially with the media and critics like Raghu smelling a rat everywhere. Thirdly, some of my former colleagues, who I think were highly loyal to me, were still working in the park, and would certainly have informed me. Lastly, it would have been virtually impossible, technically, to create a long trail of four distinct pugmarks, in exact sequence, without leaving the tell-tale footprints of the perpetrators. When Belinda once told me that she could do it, I was amazed at the credulity of the experts and activists who drive the conservation agenda of the country.

Of denial and truth

When we were reasonably certain that things in Panna were not as bad as they were made out to be, armed with these two rapid assessments, I saw an article by Bittu Sahgal, in Dainik Bhaskar, perhaps in February 2008, about the critical state of tiger conservation in the country, in which he had particularly mentioned Panna as the next Sariska, or something like that. I wrote to Bittu that he was mistaken about Panna and invited him to see things for himself. Although Bittu never came to Panna, he invited me to write a piece in the 'Debate' section of The Sanctuary Asia magazine in which he would publish my views opposite Raghu's. I readily agreed and titled my article as 'Nothing lost in Panna... So Far, while Raghu's and Joanna's piece was titled as 'Nothing is Gained By Denial' in the June 2008 edition. This article was written perhaps in February 2008 but it took time to be published. However, even before the piece was published, the park management had started reporting that there were very few tiger signs and that something had radically changed in the park. Worried at these reports, I toyed with the idea of retracting the article but could not make up my mind in time. Perhaps, I was still hoping for a turn around, before things went too far. Although the article was published, the CWLW requested the Wildlife Institute of India (WII), in May 2008, to conduct a full scale assessment to clear any doubts. WII researchers recorded the last pugmark in the park on 31st January 2009. I saw a tiger scraping on the road on 14th February, while I was there preparing for the translocation of the first tigress. That was the last sign of the native tigers of Panna then, although a DNA report that the father of the first litter of the reintroduced tigress T-2 was not the introduced male T-3, but some other tiger, indicates that some tigers were still around even after we accepted the extinction as final. However, much before the WII's report was submitted, in June 2009, we had realized that tigers had virtually vanished from the park and had reported the same to the Government of India. I became the CWLW towards the end of September 2008 and a brainstorming workshop on the situation was held in Khajuraho on 9th December 2008. A detailed status report had been sent to all concerned in May 2008 and January 2009, which admitted a sharp decline in the tiger population. Although I was accused of wrongly denying the decline of tigers in the park, my confidence, as long as it lasted, was based on first-hand information. Until November 2007, we were standing by the WII's report of 2006, and after that by NTCA's (Sen and Singh, 2008) report of January 2008, reinforced by my own impressions from the December 2007 visit.

That this confidence turned out to be misplaced will always remain painful for me, but I still cannot recall any thoughts of suppressing any information ever crossing my mind. I think the critics forget that if we had not been confident of being correct, I would not have gone to the press saying everything was fine. As I was not the CWLW then, I would have had nothing to gain by proclaiming that all was well, unless I really so believed.

The long story of accusations and denials can be summarized as follows: While Raghu and several others were saying that there were no or few tigers in the park by 2007, two *rapid* assessments confirmed that a reasonable density of tigers existed up to January 2008; the park management started reporting sharp decline in tiger signs only by April 2008; WII reported only one tiger in the park after May 2008, which disappeared towards the end of January 2009 (Wildlife Institute of India, 2009). A simplistic explanation for the situation can be that the two rapid assessments were wrong and that there were only one or two tigers in the park even in 2007. If that is correct, a major lesson for conservation is that rapid assessments are really dangerous as they can cause false comfort or alarm. However, an alternative explanation that something catastrophic happened after January 2008, has few takers, as there is no reasonable way to explain how 7-8 tigers could suddenly disappear without a trace. Although, with the advantage of hindsight, I am inclined to go with the first explanation, I think the alternative theory should not be abandoned outright, as implausible things do happen sometimes.

Poaching or emigration?

When we plotted all the tiger signs recorded by the staff on monthly maps, we found that the sign density/frequency varied widely between months. In some months the park seemed full of signs while very few signs were seen in other months. This indicated that the home ranges of tigers extended outside the park as well. If there were 7-8 male tigers in the park in January 2008 and only one tiger in May 2008, what could have happened to them during this period? This could have happened only due to sudden emigration and/or poaching. It is true, the security in the park at this time was quite weak as the infamous Thokia gang of dacoits, along with some local gangs, had taken shelter in the park by 2007 and was targeting the park staff in retaliation for some action that the park management had taken to stop cultivation of mustard in the drawdown areas of the Gangou reservoir. Poachers may have taken advantage of this situation. However, the killing of several tigers within the park would have been detected sooner or later. Mass emigration of the males from the park in search of females seems unlikely but may not be impossible. As there were virtually no females in the park, they may have received chemical signals from a faraway tigress and may just have drifted in her direction, virtually at the same time, from different parts of the park. We all have seen dozens of street dogs chasing a single female in heat. Perhaps they went outside the park after (or in search of) a female and got killed there. Tiger presence was recorded in the forests of South Panna, and adjoining districts of Chhatarpur, Damoh and Sagar, about that time, one or more of them may have been females that lured the tigers of Panna to their doom. Whether all of them died, by poaching or otherwise, in a short time, or survived to procreate there will always remain unclear. This is only a surmise, not a conclusion.

Post mortem

Two committees, one Special Investigation Team (SIT) constituted by the Government of India, and an expert committee constituted by the State, studied the extinction of tigers from Panna. Both the committees were unanimous in their conclusions that poaching, mainly outside the park, was the principal reason for the extinction (Sen et al. 2009, Dutta et al. 2009) but neither committee produced any credible evidence to show that poaching in and around Panna was any more than in other tiger-bearing areas. While the SIT said that there was no ecological reason (shortage of food and water etc.) for this extinction, the expert committee holds the skewed sex ratio, combined with repeated killing of cubs by stranger males, as an equally important reason. Both committees think that an effective buffer zone around the park could have saved the situation. While the expert committee has appreciated the steps taken to improve management and protection, such as relocation of villages, intensive patrolling, and construction of patrolling camps in sensitive locations, the SIT has interpreted the same measures differently and, strangely, has held them responsible for the tragic event. While the expert committee insists that corrective steps to improve the sex ratio should have been taken before the entire population went extinct, the SIT is totally silent on the subject. While the State's committee says that the loss was despite the best efforts of the forest department, the SIT has condemned the entire top brass of the department for failing to prevent the tragedy, while stating that there was no collusion at the local level. Interestingly, the SIT never talked to any of the senior officers of the state, although it has cast serious aspersions on their working.

In fact, the reasons, such as lack of buffer zone, alleged non-compliance with certain NTCA advisories, vacant field posts etc., for which the SIT has condemned the state, are very general and can be used to put down any state government. It was very obvious that the SIT was biased as it did not say a word about the joint responsibility of the state and the Centre in such events. NTCA is the face of tiger conservation in the country, as it controls all the resources and policy making. Therefore, its culpability in anything happening to tigers' interests should have been natural. The only reference to NTCA in the SIT report is that it gave enough money and advice to the state, without asking the state whether it was *really* adequate or not. While the expert committee avoided any adverse references to the central government, the SIT went out of its way to pass the blame to the state.

Despite these two enquiries, some vested interests and the media continued to demand a CBI enquiry into the whole episode. The department provided to the government whatever information was asked for, to facilitate such an enquiry by the CBI, but the government could never make up its mind. Perhaps the reason was that CBI investigates matters where some criminality is obvious. But in this case, no offences had been registered which the local police or the forest department had found difficult to investigate or where the police may have been biased or in complicity. The extinction of a species is a complex process in which poaching may have been a small factor compared with policy and biological issues. Therefore, despite the pressure, even from the Centre, a CBI enquiry was never ordered. In any case, the CBI enquiry might or might not have detected crimes if any had taken place, but it would not have helped in cases of systemic failures involving policies and programmes of the country.

So, what happened after all?

This is the first half of the Panna Story. The other half, the story of rebuilding the tiger population in the park, is given in the next chapter. I have told this story in as objective a manner as possible, highlighting the bare facts while keeping my own interpretations of the facts to the minimum, although it is difficult to *look* entirely objective when you yourselves are an actor in the drama. However, a mere narration of facts is pointless unless they are interpreted and interconnected to build an intelligible plot. So, how, after all, did the Panna tigers disappear? This is how it, in all likelihood, happened:

Panna National Park had an estimated 23 tigers in 1984 (Pabla 1984, unpubl.), out of which only about 10-15 should have been adults. The population was about the same size in 1996 when Raghu started his study as he recorded only 2-3 animals per 100 km^2 (Chundawat et. al. 1996-1999). The population perhaps grew only marginally, despite excellent protection, in the succeeding years, as the 2002 estimate of 29 (10—

48), (SE 3.23, cv 46.54%) over 418 km², by Karanth et al. (2004) indicates, although this estimate had a very low precision. The 2006 estimate (Jhala et al. 2008) of 8—15 tigers (SE 0.96, cv 16.8%), over 185 km², projected to 24 (15—32) over the entire tiger occupied landscape of approximately 787 km², indicates an apparent decline, but the low precision of the 2002 estimate makes the actual extent of the decline rather uncertain. The forest department's estimate of 34 or 35 tigers in 2005, must have been a gross overestimate, as WII could photograph only 8 adult tigers in the best 185 km² of the park the same year. The disappearance of these tigers after 2005, whatever the number, when the park was under global watch and the department was doing its utmost to prevent further decline, indicates that either our best was not good enough, or it was not *only* poaching that was eliminating tigers. I think both these scenarios are credible. That the latter scenario can be true, is indicated by the accepted annual turnover of tigers at 25-30% per annum. This means that approximately one third of individuals change every year, even in a stable tiger population, as a result of deaths, emigration, births and immigration. Several recent studies confirm this conclusion. 10 tigers were radio collared in Kanha in 2005 and 2006, out of which only 3 were still around in 2008, while three had been found dead, including one due to poaching. 14 tigers were photo-captured in Pench tiger reserve in 2006, out of which only 7 appeared in a repeat camera-trapping exercise in 2008 in which 12 individuals were photographed, although some of the missing tigers later returned to the area (Aniruddha Majumder, pers. com.). The same study, Shankar et al. 2013, found that the average survival rate of female tigers was only 66% per annum, while for males it was only 59%, in Pench Tiger Reserve. In Panna itself, out of 7 tigers radio collared by Raghu, only one was around after 8 years. Therefore, any tiger population can go extinct in 3-5 years, whatever its size, if there is no recruitment or immigration, poaching or no poaching. For a population to sustain removals without a crash, it needs an adequate number of breeding females. Although the WII report did not say anything about the sex ratio, conversations with Dr. Y.V. Jhala and Mr. Qamar Qureshi, the authors of the 2006 report, indicated an unhealthy sex ratio of fewer females than males. Only one cub was reported in the discredited 2005 departmental census. After the poisoning of a tigress, along with its two sub-adult female cubs, in May 2006, this population had no tigresses or cubs. Raghu suspected, in February 2004, the killing of at least three litters by males competing for females and prime space in the previous one year. Obviously, the foundation of this extinction was laid by this infanticide and the death of the last breeding female in 2006. As there was no recruitment after 2005, it is obvious that, by 2008, there should be very few animals in the area, as approximately 75-90% of the animals would have disappeared by then, as a result of the natural turnover of the species. Therefore, the extinction of the species by 2009 should not be surprising. If locals were reporting only one or two animals in 2007, while assessments by experts indicated 7-8 animals, obviously the latter were wrong. Even my own assessment of December 2007, when two animals were *actually* seen, among other evidence, must have been an error of judgment. How the last few tigers died is immaterial, as they would, in any case, have died without procreating, if they had stayed in the park. As no carcasses were found within the park, it is likely that they also died, in due course, outside the park, either on regular forays, or looking for a distant, elusive, mate. Whether any of the tigers reported in the adjoining Chhatarpur, Damoh, Sagar and Satna districts around that time were the Panna animals will never be known, but it is possible that some of them may have been the elusive tigers of Panna. The capture of the translocated male T-3 nearly 200 km away from Panna in Damoh district in 2009, and the recovery of the sub-adult male cub of the translocated tigress T-1 in the Singhpur range of Satna district, nearly 100 km away from the park, in July 2012, prove that tigers can wander over large distances. One radio collared male cub of T-2 wandered into Uttar Pradesh and never returned. It was captured and translocated to Satpura Tiger Reserve in January 2013. Similarly, another male drifted towards Sidhi district and was helped along, by translocation, to reach Sanjay Tiger Reserve in early 2014.

Did they all die outside the park?

Both the enquiry committees concur that the deaths of the Panna tigers, between 2005 and 2008, must have happened outside the park, as the park itself was believed to be really well protected, at least during this period. I think this is a convenient fallacy which everybody seems to have readily accepted. We all have seen poaching of all kinds of animals taking place in the best protected areas. In fact, our protected areas are almost as vulnerable as any other forest area, despite their name, primarily because of their open boundaries. Even the army and the BSF are unable to check the infiltration by sundry terrorists and smugglers, often in the easiest of terrains, despite the virtually impregnable border fences, lighting, observation posts, intensive patrolling, intelligence, weapons and the license to shoot. It is anybody's guess how an underfunded and underequipped forest department, staffed mostly with aging and demotivated guards, can defend a porous and unfenced park, with difficult terrain and nearly opaque, dense forests. The last tigress in Panna was poisoned within the park in 2006 and another young tigress born to reintroduced tigress T-2, which died in July 2012 within the park, was most likely poisoned. We have had tigers killed by poachers inside Kanha and Bandhavgarh. It is true that the carcasses of some of the tigers would have been detected, if all the tigers, at least 8-15, had been killed inside the park after 2006, but, if the tigers were killed for smuggling their skins and bones, the poachers could have removed the bodies without detection. Moreover, the presence of vindictive dacoit gangs in the park at this critical juncture must have rendered unarmed patrolling impossible. Therefore, it is likely that the tigers were killed both within and outside the park, despite better security inside, although the chances of their deaths outside are marginally higher.

Not being able to prevent or detect poaching, especially that of tigers, is one thing, but suppression of poaching cases by the authorities can be the worst of crimes. I have never known any officer deliberately suppressing any serious crime cases, just to avoid being held responsible. However, when Mr. R. Srinivasmurthy, the field director, submitted a report indicating several cases of deliberate suppression of poaching cases by his predecessors, I was shattered beyond belief. He said the matter was so serious that it should be investigated by a high powered committee of senior police and forest officers. I read the report in utter shock and sent my able colleague Mr. Tilak Raj Sharma APCCF to do a preliminary inquiry before taking any further action. He found no substance in the claims as the records of necessary action were available in Mr. Murthy's office itself. The most worrying case was that of a preliminary offence report (POR), found in the stolen bag of a forest guard, showing the seizure of two tiger skins. The POR was mailed by the thief to the then field director, asking for action. Mr. Murthy had got the signatures of the forest guard verified by a hand writing expert and was convinced that it was a case which the then field director had suppressed deliberately. However, it turned out that the forest guard had kept a signed but blank POR form in the bag which was stolen and the thief, who had some score to settle with the forest guard, entered all the details himself and sent the POR to the field director in the hope that he would have his revenge. The case had been marked for investigation but we did not find any report in the file. When I noticed the residence of the accused mentioned in the document as Satna, while the beat guard was posted in a beat in Chhatarpur district (perhaps Sukwaha beat), I became curious how he could seize tiger skins in another district, nowhere near his beat. I was relieved when we came to know that the accused mentioned in the POR was the guard's own brother! Mr. Murthy's report remained in the news and gave us some serious headache. But, in the end, I was relieved that some of my esteemed colleagues had come out unblemished from this episode.

Why only males survived?

Why there were only males in the population, towards the end, is difficult to explain. Raghu believes females are relatively more prone to poaching as they are easy to detect when with cubs, and because they tend to kill more livestock to feed their young, and consequently get poisoned. H.S. Panwar believes that the tigresses may have migrated to the periphery, or the risky buffer, of the park, to protect themselves and their young from males competing for females and prime territories, and got poached (Dutta et al. 2010). However, without disputing these theories, I have a third hypothesis. It is that, just by sheer coincidence, more male cubs were born during that period than the females, and the few female cubs that were born did not survive to adulthood, again coincidentally. That this can happen is evident from our experience with the introduced tigers in Panna itself. Out of the 17 cubs born to the first three introduced tigresses, 12 were male and 3 were females, while two died before their sex could be determined. Out of the 12 males, 10 were still in the park, while one had been shifted to Kanha for captive rearing as it was abandoned by its mother only a few days after its birth, and another was translocated to Satpura Tiger Reserve. Out of the 3 females, one was found dead and its cause of death is still unknown while another was killed and eaten by other tigers, including its own mother. If we had no more breeding females, this new population would also have been on its way to doom, with 10 males and only one female offspring, within 2-3 years of showing signs of a turn around. We can imagine what would have been the situation today if the tigress with two sub-adult female cubs had not died in 2006. The three of them would have given birth to 6-12 cubs over the next two three years and we would have had 7-8 tigers in the park even in 2009! Obviously, the survival or demise of a single breeding tigress would have changed the course of history. But then we would not have learned what we have done. We now know how to recreate wild tiger populations from a scratch!

Did we miss anything?

Whether poaching was the principal factor in this extinction or only a contributory factor will always remain a mystery, but the moot question is whether we could have done anything more than what was done to prevent poaching in the park. There is always scope for improvement, and the efficacy of the anti-poaching activities could, perhaps, have been marginally improved. Still, despite the advantage of considerable hindsight, I have not been able to think of a single thing which we missed. Although we were unlucky to have some infamous, allegedly revengeful, dacoits occupying the park during the critical period, which must have made our staff jittery and reduced their effectiveness, we had all the classical anti-poaching apparatus in place all the time. Although the SIT has found several faults with the park management, perhaps because they had to defend NTCA, they did so by deliberately ignoring the contrary evidence. I am very sure that if poaching can happen in Panna tiger reserve, under those circumstances, then it is not the failure of the management of an individual park management alone, but it is the failure of the prevalent conservation model itself. I believe several things have contributed to this failure not all of which can be thrown at the local or state level managers.

Lessons from Panna

Events like Panna's tiger extinction can perhaps be prevented if we follow a different approach to conservation illustrated in the following discussion:

Parks and fences

The primary factor in this saga has been our obsession with open boundaries for our protected areas. As discussed above, it is virtually impossible to call an area protected without effective fencing or boundary walls. There is no way an open boundary, running over hundreds of kilometres, over difficult terrain often with hostile neighbours, can be protected by a ragtag collection of primarily casual labour, who far outnumber the regular staff in most parks. If poachers can get into the parks, as they often do, and tigers can go out and get killed, calling them 'protected areas' sounds like a joke. We keep our boundaries open in the hope that animals spilling over from protected areas will be able to occupy the adjoining forests and can perhaps disperse into the larger landscapes, making genetic exchange between metapopulations possible. But this has not happened in the last fifty years of our pursuit of this madness, except some rare tigers moving from one PA to another, and is unlikely to happen in future. How many tigers die when one animal manages to cross the dangerous corridor is anybody's guess. It is high time that we call a halt to this fancy and make our park managers accountable for their jobs after giving them reasonable control of the area through proper fencing. On the basis of a comparative study of the management approaches and population trends of lions, in 42 sites across 11 countries in Africa, a team of 58 scientists (Packer et al. 2013) found that, "Lion populations in fenced reserves are significantly closer to their estimated carrying capacities than unfenced populations. Whereas fenced reserves can maintain lions at 80% of their potential densities on annual management budgets of $ 500/km^{-2}, unfenced populations require budgets in excess of $2000/km^{-2} to attain half their potential densities. ... Nearly half the unfenced lion populations may decline to near extinction over the next 20–40 years." If we follow this single, sensible, recommendation from world's best scientists, life will be much easier for all of us, including tigers.

A pair of wild tigers were translocated to Satkosia Tiger Reserve of Odisha, from MP, recently, as a part of a reintroduction project. The project was undertaken despite the opposition from local people. Unfortunately, the tigress killed two persons and was captured in September 2018. The male was found dead a few days later, reportedly after suffering grievous injuries in a poacher's snare. The blame game has begun and it is curtains for the project for now. Although there may be many management failures which led to this situation (e.g. Satkosia has no trained elephants which can be used to control tiger movements), a fence around the park would certainly have saved the victims, tigers, as well as this project. NTCA has expectedly thrown all the blame on the state, while nobody is questioning why NTCA gave a go ahead to such an ill-conceived project.

Erratic staffing policies

The shortage of field staff, especially of the right quality, is another major hurdle in effective conservation. The shortage is not because the government does not want to fill the vacancies. It is because the rate of retirements in the department, for the last ten years or so, has been so rapid that the state has not been able to recruit staff at the same pace. All this due to faulty staffing policies put in place decades ago. The state recruited a lot of staff in the nineteen seventies and early eighties, when forest working (felling) was nationalized. In the nineties, the State placed a complete ban on recruitments as it could not afford the salaries. While almost no recruitments to middle and higher levels had taken place since the mid-eighties, most new forest guards have come from the ranks of "daily wagers' who were already quite old. As a result, nearly all the workforce, including the officers, were nearing retirement in the last decade and were virtually unfit for strenuous field work. We can imagine the state of affairs from the fact that the same officers who were managing the parks as deputy conservators in the nineties were still managing them as chief conservators more than twenty years later, with their culminating personal responsibilities and reduced fitness. The moral of the story is that long term manpower planning of the department should in no case be tinkered with to tide over some immediate problems.

Need for proactive conservation

We often treat anti-poaching action as being synonymous with wildlife management, as Project Tiger was primarily founded on the premise that nature should be left alone. This is a fundamentally flawed premise as wild animals are ecologically linked with each other in the form of a food web, and through ecological processes such as competition. Nature, left to itself, is incapable of maintaining a balance between the populations of competing species in the short term. As a result, if we do not intervene, some species can be wiped out while others may outgrow the limits of the available habitat. Therefore, wildlife populations have to be managed to favour the endangered and vulnerable species at the cost of more abundant life forms. Moreover, the defects in the structure of small populations have to be corrected to enable them to tide over accidental or inherent problems. Panna tigers are a case in point. It was known all along that the population was short on females and an obvious solution would have been to introduce a few females into the population. But as translocation or introduction of wild animals is not the culture here, we kept hesitating, in the hope that the females would appear from somewhere on their own, until it was too late. If we had a culture of active management of wildlife, the history of Panna may have been different. Our experience in the reintroduction of tigers, gaur and blackbuck in their former domains since the Panna debacle clearly proves that leaving nature alone is not enough for preserving wildlife: nature and man have to work together to preserve our biodiversity.

Buffer zone: a panacea?

One more issue on which both the enquiry committees have agreed is the need for an 'effective buffer zone' for the park. They believed that if the surrounding forests had been under the control of the field director, the tigers that migrated there would have been safer. Although this is a very popular and tempting hypothesis, I think this too is flawed, in the present context. The concept of buffer zones has been around ever since Project Tiger came into the country, but the buffer zones have mostly acted as the veritable sinks for the animals spilling out of the core areas. Most of the recorded cases of tiger poaching in Kanha have happened in the buffer zone, which is under the control of the same field director. It must be the same in other reserves too. There are several reasons for this. The primary reason is that usually the buffer zone becomes a poor cousin of the core area, even poorer than the adjoining forest divisions, as it lacks the glamour and resources synonymous with the core. It gets poorer quality staff and other resources, often what is not required in the core. Buffer zone management is a much more complex and resource intensive discipline than the management of the core, as it involves meeting the livelihood and other needs of the people, in addition to anti-poaching and forest management. The country neither has the skills nor the resources to do this. NTCA tends to provide minimal resources to the buffer zones, whatever it can spare after meeting the needs of the core areas. Generally, little is left for the buffer zones. Interestingly, Kanha buffer used to get close to Rupees eight million per year around the year 2000 while the allocation came down to approx. Rs. two million by 2007-08. Over the same time, the allocations to the core area grew to Rs. 40-50 million per annum. The allocation to the Kanha buffer improved when we brought this conundrum to the notice of the NTCA, but were nowhere near the requirement, or what the core received. In fact, we have almost forgotten the human side of the buffer zone management, the purpose for which the concept of buffer zones was primarily invented. We are now demanding buffer zones primarily to expand the security umbrella around the core areas. This has not worked so far, and is definitely not going to work in future, as our current thinking of a protectionist approach to buffer zone management is fundamentally flawed. Buffer zones were primarily meant to enhance the stakes of the neighbouring communities in conservation through conservation-linked livelihoods and ecodevelopment. As we have no money for ecodevelopment, and as wildlife tourism, the only vocation that can bring them sustainable livelihoods, is also an anathema to the powers that be, our buffer zones will continue to be the conservation sinks that they are now.

Panna now has a buffer zone, notified under pressure from NTCA and the Supreme Court. Let us hope it lives up to the fancy of the country.

CHAPTER 3

Resurrection of Panna Tigers

Background

The unique success of the tiger reintroduction programme in Panna is well known by now as many reports and papers have already documented how this monumental success was achieved. However, the world knows only one half of the story as the behind-the-scenes struggle, which actually made it all happen, is not a part of the technical papers being published. Not many people know that the project almost got scrapped more than once, for completely specious reasons, before it reached its well-known culmination. If we had accepted these setbacks, the Panna story would have been entirely different. It was only dogged pursuit and relentless pressure from the State, on GoI and NTCA, which finally ensured the recovery of Panna. Therefore, it is worthwhile to review the events which shaped the destiny of this project so that future generations can learn some useful lessons in the administration of conservation.

Here is the gripping story from one of the actors in this drama.

The year 2007 was the watershed year in the history of Panna National Park as it was this year that the department started admitting that there was a problem with the tiger population of the park. Until then, the debate was about the number of tigers, not about whether they were at all there or not. Although there were shouts from several quarters that the decline in Panna was much worse than what was reported by WII, the department was, perhaps justifiably, confident that nothing out of the ordinary had happened in Panna until then. We also felt rather secure in the belief that enough strengthening of the park management had been done, 2005 onwards, to ensure recovery of the population, even if there had indeed been a decline in tiger population. But the expected recovery did not materialise.Although the department did not accept that the park had lost its tigers further since the assessment by WII, the park management had started noticing the complete absence of tigresses and cubs in the park by 2007.

Build up to the translocation

Based on these observations, thoughts of bringing in one or two females from other parks, to reinforce the population, had started crossing our minds. Immediately after the translocation of tigers to Sariska, NTCA adopted a *sou moto* resolution to translocate two tigresses to Panna, in March 2008.

However, tigers can be captured for translocation only with prior permission of the MOEF&CC, as provided in section 12 of the WLPA, for which a formal proposal has to be submitted. In May 2008, a project proposal was sent to GoI and NTCA to permit the translocation of two tigresses to Panna from other parks of the state. About the same time, the park management started reporting a steep decline in the tiger signs and sightings in the park and the department invited WII to make another assessment of the situation. The MOEF&CC permission for translocating two tigresses came in October 2008; the NTCA approved the project in December 2008 while the funds were released by NTCA only towards the end of March 2009. In the meantime, we had gone ahead with the preparations for the implementation of the project with state funding, after receiving MoEF&CC permission, and had an enclosure, for keeping the translocated tigresses for a few days, built in Badgadi by the end of February 2009. Target animals for translocation, one each from Bandhavgarh and Kanha, had also been identified. WII had finished its assessment by then and had declared that they recorded the photographs of only one tiger in the park since May 2008, which too had disappeared by the end of February 2009. So, the tiger translocation programme which was conceived as a *supplementation* or *reinforcement* programme, ended up being a *reintroduction* programme.

The reintroduction of tigers in Sariska had already started in 2008 and we were expected to follow the same template. They had airlifted their tigers from Ranthambhore to Sariska and had kept them in a one-hectare enclosure for about a week before releasing them into the park. So, we also built an enclosure and approached the Indian Air Force (IAF) to lend their helicopters for airlifting the tigresses from Kanha and Bandhavgarh. Although we did not believe that the enclosure or airlifting were necessary, as we had always transported tigers over 400–500 km by road, we did not want to deviate from the Sariska template, as we were already under pressure for not following some of NTCA's advisories. However, the IAF readily agreed to our request, which was also supported by a letter from the Minister for Environment and Forests. Perhaps having the Defence Secretary from the MP cadre also helped in securing the IAF support. However, they could not send the chopper for the first translocation from Bandhavgarh.

Which tigers to translocate?

An interesting controversy developed while we were discussing the translocation project. I had directed the Field Directors of Kanha, Bandhavgarh and Pench tiger reserves to identify suitable animals for translocation. The criteria given to them were that the candidate animal should:

a. be approximately 4 years old;

b. be from a large litter, preferably consisting of 4 siblings, so that it has the potential of producing large litters in Panna;

c. not be an isolated animal but, rather, be an animal which is vying for space with its siblings or mother, so that its removal does not create a vacuum in the population.

Naturally it had to be from an area with high tiger density.

I was also keen to take a young mother, rather than a virgin tigress, that would have given me the assurance that the animal had no gynaecological or other breeding problem. However, I did not pursue this idea as it would have reduced our choices. I also knew that the purists would hate me even more if I disturbed the existing land tenures of tigers.

But when the NTCA approval for the project came in December 2008, it came with the condition that the animals to be translocated should be dispersing animals, approximately two years old, preferably from the buffer zone. By then we had already identified candidate animals, one each in the core areas of Kanha and Bandhavgarh. Changing the selection at this stage would have delayed the project until the following year, as we were already heading into the hot summer. We wrote to NTCA in this regard, but before our differences could be resolved the two tigresses had been translocated. Although this was only a minor deviation, our critics and the press made quite an issue of our *violation* of the NTCA guidelines, and it became one of the main planks on which people tried to stall the project later.

All hell breaks loose

After considerable homework, we had identified the two tigresses to be translocated. But when it came to capturing the animals, local interest groups were up in arms. The lodge owners, guides, and tour operators felt that their businesses would suffer if a tiger was removed from *their* park. So much so that a former forest minister also threatened me of riots if we picked up any tiger from Pench. The tigress to be removed from Bandhavgarh was really a well-known animal, quite tolerant of vehicles and elephants. We started receiving representations and phone calls that we should not remove any animal from *their* park or else there would be an agitation. When the IAF informed us that they would not be able to provide the helicopter on the 3rd of March 2009, the day of translocation from Bandhavgarh, we were really worried that these people would try to block the road. However, everything went off smoothly, as we picked up the animal at about 6.00 pm and drove away very quickly, before people could get ready to protest. One person had filed a PIL in the High Court and was trying to obtain a stay on the operation. The day we picked up the tigress from Kanha, Sunday, the 9th of March 2009, the court hearing was in progress at the residence of the judge and we kept praying that we would be able to finish our operation before the court proceedings concluded; fortunately the court did not grant the injunction.

The operation in Kanha was in fact planned for the 8th of March but we could do it only on the 9th. I was still in Panna after releasing the Bandhavgarh tigress, now known as T-1, on the 6th of March, when I received word that the target animal in Kanha was available. I started for Kanha the same afternoon and arrived on the morning of the 7th to find that the target animal had vanished after feeding on a gaur carcass till midday. Next day there was no sign of the animal, while the IAF helicopter was waiting, and the agitation against the translocation was building up. Local guides held a demonstration at the park gate and local politicians, including a minister who otherwise always treated the park, and the tigers, as a menace, came to convince me to call off the operation, or else. I was worried that even if I ignored the threats, I might get orders from Bhopal to call it off. Fortunately we were able to brave the tense day without any major problem, except that I had an uncomfortable night thinking that we might have to call the operation off, in any case, if the target animal was not located soon. There was no sign of the target animal next morning and I was inclined to allow the chopper to go back when, around 11.00 am, the word came that a sister of the target animal, from the same litter, had been located in the Indri grassland. This animal had not been seen for nearly six months and was believed to be a very shy and reclusive animal. As she also met all the selection criteria, we picked her up and airlifted her to Panna by lunch. The fact that we had actually captured the *wrong* animal leaked to the press immediately and it became another piece of evidence against us in the ongoing media trial of the department, of CWLW in particular.

Big guns fire at us

The translocation of these two tigresses was planned to restart breeding in a tiger population devoid of females. But, as mentioned before, by the time the females arrived, there were no males in the area. Therefore, we now needed at least one male tiger in the park. Moreover, the entire strategy had to be recast as the job now was to recreate a tiger population from scratch, rather than adding a few animals into an existing population. Therefore, we obtained the permission from NTCA and

MoEF&CC to take one male and two more females from other parks to Panna.

But before any further action could be taken, all hell broke loose as prominent conservationists of the country, namely, Valmik Thapar, Belinda Wright, P.K. Sen, Brijendra Singh, Raghu Chundawat and Ullas Karanth, wrote a letter to the Prime Minister, Chief Minister, and to everyone else that mattered, that the reintroduction programme was a cover up for the mismanagement of the park by the department and that it was being undertaken in violation of the directives of NTCA and GoI, and that it should be halted forthwith, along with fixing responsibility for the loss of the tiger population from the park. I could never understand the motives behind the opposition to the tiger reintroduction programme, by the very people who had been driving the conservation bandwagon in the country for long, especially at this stage when two tigresses had already been transferred. In fact, Valmik and Raghu had supported translocation in a meeting with NTCA, provided Raghu was made a member of the committee to supervise the work. Unfortunately, we could not do so as his case against us was still pending in the court. Raghu had even called me to expedite the translocation of the male, after the two females had been introduced. Criticism of the department or of the individual officers for letting the tigers disappear was understandable. Criticism of the reintroduction programme, if it had failed, would also have been justified. But why these worthies opposed the reintroduction, per se, will always remain a mystery to me. Perhaps it was because of an unfulfilled desire to occupy the centre-stage in this game-changing endeavour!

Government of India had already constituted an SIT to find out whether there was any collusion by the park staff in the (presumed) poaching of the tigers, while the Government of MP had also constituted its own Expert Committee to study the causes of this extinction and to recommend steps to prevent such incidences in future. The SIT found no staff collusion in any poaching cases, but went beyond its mandate to blame the entire top brass of the department for this debacle. The state's own expert committee concluded that the extinction happened despite the best efforts of the state, due to several reasons, including poaching. The press latched on to the letter of the big guns and screamed for blood every day. As is their wont, the politicians wilted under pressure, despite having appreciated our work repeatedly. So, heads had to roll and mine was the only one still available for sacrifice, as all others, the PCCFs, CWLW and Principal Secretaries had already retired or had moved on long ago. So, I was transferred out in August 2009. Directors of all the major parks, including those who had just joined, were also changed just to show that the government was dead serious.

Fortunately, I was brought back in June 2010. As I was the principal architect of the reintroduction programme, the world was wondering whether it would reach its logical end in my absence or not. Happily, we showed the world that the systems are as important in government as individuals. Before I returned as the CWLW, a male tiger had already been translocated from Pench after a month-long effort and another month of hard work in retrieving it from its homing journey back to Pench. The programme had also acquired its first stamp of success by then, as T-1, the first translocated tigress, had delivered its first litter of four, sired by the runaway male T-3, in April 2010.

One major charge against us was that we had undertaken the reintroduction project in an ad-hoc manner without following the standard protocol. Everyone forgot that GoI, NTCA and WII had approved the action plan and had imposed their own conditions. WII scientists were actually on the team that captured and translocated the animals. No one, outside the MP Forest Department (MPFD), told the critics that we were all in it together. The critics did not want to believe that we must have done our homework well, although I had gone over virtually every word written on the subject before embarking on this journey. As there was no standard protocol for translocating tigers, *per se*, WII was asked to draft a protocol and a committee of the bigwigs of conservation approved it. I was wondering, all along, what new wisdom they would put in this protocol, as the famous IUCN guidelines for reintroductions had been there forever and we had followed them to the last comma and full stop. In any case, perhaps just to please the lobbies, the protocol was issued but it was nothing but the IUCN guidelines in a new jacket. Suffice it to say that we followed this protocol assiduously, without ever reading it seriously. And no one faulted us on this count again.

NTCA and WII block the making of history

In the meantime, a new reintroduction plan, involving four females and two males, had been approved by GoI. When it came to getting two more tigresses for Panna, we found it difficult to get the animals as per our exact specifications. But we were even more worried about the opposition from various interests we had faced earlier. Coincidentally, we had two tigresses in an enclosure in Kanha and I started weighing the possibility of using these animals for the Panna programme. Over the next few sleepless nights, my mind was made. These animals had been orphaned when approximately 15 days old, back in 2005 and had been brought up in captivity since then; they were already five years old and had already been feeding on wild spotted deer in a large enclosure for nearly two years. These animals, along with a male sibling, had been brought up with the objective of releasing them back in the wild, in Kanha, someday. Initially they were hand-reared by a single handler, slowly they were shifted to a diet of dressed chicken and goat meat. But at about the age of three years, the females were transferred to a large enclosure, about 7 ha in size, and were fed on live, wild prey. Spotted deer were driven into their enclosure very ingeniously, with the help of trap gates, from time to time. Nobody was allowed near the enclosure, which had its fence covered with grass mats, except the people monitoring their behaviour from a hide. Even I had not seen them till I got interested in them for the Panna programme. By 2010 they had already killed and eaten more than 300 spotted deer and it was becoming more and more difficult to feed them, as the surrounding chital population had become wary of the trap gates. Kanha management was pressing us for a final decision regarding their future due to this difficulty. I was not ready to release them in Kanha, as, we all agreed, they had little chance to survive in competition with existing tigers. The male had already been shifted to Van

Vihar zoo in Bhopal, when it was approximately 3 years old, as it was thought that there were plenty of males in Kanha. Despite never having been given a chance to kill wild prey in the Kanha enclosure, this male killed a spotted deer within minutes of its release into its pen in Van Vihar. The two females, adept at killing spotted deer by now, seemed ideal to me for this programme, despite several concerns. I believed that we would lose nothing if they did not take to the new environment successfully and that they would have served no purpose for conservation if they stayed in a zoo all their lives. Obviously their success in surviving and procreating in Panna had the potential to open completely new avenues for conservation. In my opinion, they had much better chances of success in Panna than in Kanha because of a far lower tiger density in Panna.

So, we requested NTCA to approve their translocation to Panna and copied the proposal to WII, as was the practice. WII immediately shot the proposal down, saying that these tigers stood no chance of survival in the wild. Field Director Panna, Mr. Srinivasmurthy, also did not want to risk a failure and wrote to me against the move. NTCA did not respond to our proposal for releasing these tigresses in Panna, but, inexplicably, cancelled our existing permission for further translocations, for no obvious reason, except that we had "not implemented the project for more than eight months since the permission was granted"! All this while my worries were mounting with the fear that the only male tiger might again wander away in search of receptive females, as the two available females, having already littered, were not likely to come into oestrus for a year or so. As we know, the previous few native males were believed to have left the park, towards the end of 2008, perhaps because there were no females to keep them tied to the place.

Minister comes to the rescue

I had almost abandoned the programme in despair, but fate had willed it differently. I happened to run into the then Minister for Environment and Forests, Mr. Jairam Ramesh, in the corridors of Paryavaran Bhawan, the offices of MOEF&CC in Delhi. He knew that I was not happy with the way his Ministry was treating us, especially our zeal for new initiatives, and immediately invited me to his room for a chat. I asked for a few minutes, but, by the time I reached his office, he had already left for Patna and had left word that he would call me to Delhi soon. However, before he could invite me to Delhi, I met him in his office and opened my heart to him. One of the points I pressed was that the naturalization, in Panna, of these two tigresses would be easier than that of any fully wild tigresses and that the project had the potential to change the way conservation is done in India and the world. He promised to look into the matter and, on his next visit to Bhopal, brought Dr. Rajesh Gopal, Member Secretary of NTCA, with him. We had a meeting in my office and I implored him to let this project, and the stalled gaur translocation in Bandhavgarh, go ahead. I do not know what the minister had told Rajesh, but he readily agreed. We even agreed on some phony correspondence to assist him in justifying the reversal of NTCA's position on the issue. We had another meeting in Delhi, in which Rajesh was very supportive, WII faculty was divided, but the decision to carry out the translocation of the two tigresses was taken, and the rest is history. Obviously, we owe the success of this project largely to the venerable Mr. Jairam Ramesh! I, like many others, wish he had stayed in our ministry some more time.

When I was running from pillar to post to open the doors for the continuation of this project, with this new orientation, several well-wishers advised me to calm down and spend the last year or so of my career comfortably. I had lost my job once and was putting my head on the line again. No one really believed that the idea would work. They failed to understand why I was risking my career and reputation and was not just enjoying the success we had already achieved. But, somehow, my madness refused to abate, so convinced was I of the value of this move.

Orphans open new doors to tiger conservation

We had planned to capture the two tigresses on 30 December 2010. But when we arrived for the operation, we found that the tigresses had fought with each other a day or two before and had bruises and injuries on several parts of their bodies. Naturally, releasing injured tigresses in the wild was not advisable. So, we had to delay the operation after inspecting the animals and giving a dart full of antibiotics to each. We had all along believed that releasing both the siblings together in Panna would be better as they would have the tendency to stick together, at least in the beginning, in an unknown place, making it easier to monitor and manage them even if the radio collars failed. However, it dawned on us that managing two tigresses simultaneously would have been extremely difficult if they did not stay together during the exploration of the new habitat, especially if one of them decided to go back to Kanha, like the male, and the other in some other direction. Thus, this delay came as a blessing in disguise, and we decided to release the second tigress only after the first one had fully settled. So, we picked up only one of the tigresses, now called T-4, on 27 March 2011, and released it in Panna the next morning, without using the enclosure. It gave birth to two cubs perhaps in December 2011 or January 2012. Tigress T-5, the sister of T-4, was moved on November 13, 2011, after T-4 seemed to have fully settled in its new domain. As we had prophesied to NTCA and WII, the settlement of the captive tigresses seemed to be much easier and quicker than the wild tigresses, as their daily movements continued to be very limited, perhaps due to the fact that they had not seen the world beyond the seven hectares in which they had lived all their adult lives.

Our worries about the orphans

It is not that we did not have any concerns about the fate of these animals in the wild. In fact we had several major concerns about them and tried to address them, as best as possible, before release, as well as after. For example:

(a) We were worried that they might associate human presence with food, and be thus prone to dangerous interaction with people after release, because they had been hand-fed when they were babies. Even later, there were obvious signs of a human hand, like trap doors opening and closing or people shouting and whispering, when prey was introduced into their enclosure, although we tried to make the human presence around their enclosure as unobtrusive as possible;

(b) As food had always been provided to them, we were worried that they may have got into the habit of waiting for food to be brought to them, as in the enclosure, rather than going in search of it;

(c) We were also not sure whether the hunting skills shown by them in the enclosure were adequate to support them in the wild. We feared that they might find it difficult to capture and kill a truly free-ranging animal without the fence which they must have learnt to use as an aid in hunting in the enclosure;

(d) We were wondering whether they would treat animals other than spotted deer also as food because they had fed only on this deer in the enclosure, except a few domestic pigs and buffalo calves given to them precisely for this reason;

(e) We were not sure whether they had any fear of man as they had all along been supported by men.

(f) Lastly, we wondered how they would react to the world outside their enclosure, with vehicles, elephants and humans all around them, especially in the initial phases when they would have to be managed.

Preparations for the new life

Towards the end of their captivity, when we had set our eyes on them as potential candidates for Panna, we had started preparing them for their future, beyond just hunting training. We removed the thatch cladding from the fence so that they could see the world outside, with other animals, including tigers, men and vehicles, moving around. We tried to make them comfortable with our working elephants as much as possible as elephants were going to be a major tool for monitoring and managing their movements in Panna. Although it might sound ridiculous now, we even tried to inculcate some fear of humans in them. For that I asked the local staff to shout at them, menacingly, and throw sticks or pebbles at them, threateningly, whenever they passed by the enclosure. How much of this was actually done and whether all this had a role in shaping their behaviour is not certain, but we saw nothing odd in these animals at all. They took very little time to settle down. They were seen mating with the resident male as soon as they had learnt to feed themselves. T-4 delivered two litters within three years, although T-5 delivered her first litter almost after two years, despite frequently mating with T-3. By the time I heard the happy news in the summer of 2013, I had started feeling that perhaps I was right in thinking that we should use breeding tigresses, rather than virgins, as founder animals, to eliminate the risk of having to deal with an animal with gynaecological problems. Fortunately, that premise is still to be validated!

Many bogeys

While everything was going so well, our critics and media were scouring the universe for some new ammunition to attack us. They said that these tigers can never be the *Panna* tigers, as the *Bundela* genes had already been lost. I hope the fact that WII has found that the tigers in Kanha, Melghat (Maharashtra) and Ranthambhore (Rajasthan) are related and that the Wildlife Conservation Society (WCS) has found that tiger genes are still travelling from Pench to Nagarjun Sagar (Andhra Pradesh) should comfort their souls a little. A discovery that the genes of the cubs of T-2 did not match the genome of T-3 means that some other male from the original Panna stock was still lurking somewhere in the shadows.

We, in MP, were lucky to have several source populations for translocation; therefore the *inbreeding* bogey could not halt our progress. By the time the search for a male was mounted, this bogey had raised its head in the case of Sariska, despite open knowledge that most tiger populations are highly inbred, by their very nature, small numbers and demography. We, too, had to abandon a male that had been selected in Bandhavgarh, in favour of the one from Pench (now the famous T-3). If we had limited choice, we would perhaps have been lynched for promoting incest among tigers.

We were also lucky to be able to select the founder animals as per our own criteria rather than allowing someone else's pseudoscience to influence us. When people asked me why Panna filled up so quickly while Sariska continued to struggle for a long time, I used to tell them that the founder animals made the difference, apart from luck. As all our founders were ready to breed, we did not have to wait long to hear the good news. Furthermore, all our initial litters were of four each. In contrast, the Sariska founders took time to mature and deliver the results, and were not selected on the basis of their ancestral fecundity.

Despite the resounding success of the reintroduction programme, people, strangely, associate the park more with its past failures. So much so, that Dr. Rajesh Gopal, who has done so much for tiger conservation in the country, refused to sign the certificates of appreciation for the Panna staff, when he accompanied Mr. Jairam Ramesh to Panna in the summer of 2011. I do not know what he meant by, "What will people say?" Quite embarrassed, the minister had to assure the staff that he would send them certificates under his own signatures, which he promptly did on his return to Delhi.

Panna is the new beacon

Panna has made history on several counts. It lost its entire tiger population, despite being consistently rated as one of the better managed tiger reserves of the country. Poaching must have played a major role, at some stage, in this debacle, but it does not explain the entire sequence of events. However, we can get some satisfaction from the fact that if we had not lost all the tigers in Panna, the world would never have learnt that even tigers can be reintroduced if suitable habitat is available. Even more significant is the lesson that tigers raised in captivity can also be trained to survive and procreate in the wild. If we continue to have 'protected' areas with porous boundaries, where poachers can sneak in and animals can go out and get killed, populations are certainly going to continue to go extinct in future. But these extinctions, though always costly and painful, need not be permanent now, as the Panna story can light up the way for reversing them. We already hear reports of Kazakhstan, Russia and Cambodia being interested in learning from our debacle and redemption. Let us pray the failed Satkosia project (see previous chapter) will only be a minor dampener on the new conservation road!

CHAPTER 4

Gaur Returns to Bandhavgarh

Background

Preservation of wildlife in a poor and populous country is a very complex and difficult task. Species have been dwindling ever since records have been maintained, especially in densely populated countries. Extinctions of wild animals generally follow a common pattern: species first become extinct locally and, over time, the areas of extinction enlarge and coalesce to make the extinctions regional, national or global. Although local extinctions can happen due to natural or ecological reasons, most extinctions are caused by human expansion into wildlife habitats and the overexploitation of animals. Preservation of wild animals generally involves a three pronged approach: protection of the animals against overexploitation or poaching; protection or restoration of their habitat; and reintroduction of the depleted species in its old habitat if the habitat is still intact. However, in India, conservation efforts have generally been limited to anti-poaching and habitat protection and very few efforts have been made to reintroduce a species after its local extinction. The only two exceptions have been the introduction of the rhino in Dudhwa National Park, which still lives in a fenced enclosure, and the gharial (*Gavialis gangeticus*) in some rivers, in the eighties of the last century, apart from the failed and forgotten attempt to introduce lions in the Chandraprabha sanctuary of Uttar Pradesh in 1957.

I have long been uncomfortable with the fact that we have been losing species after species even from our protected areas. We lost the gaur (*Bos gaurus*) from Bandhavgarh, blackbuck (*Antelope cervicapra*) from Kanha and the great Indian bustard (*Ardeotis nigriceps)* from Karera sanctuary in the nineties, while we lost the tiger from Panna more recently. There may be several other unrecorded extinctions as well. For example, no one has noticed the absence of gaur from Sanjay National Park, although they were there in the eighties. Several years ago, I had started thinking that if the PAs are not protecting the endangered species, they are not worth so much expense. An obvious course, where a serious decline in a population is noticed, should have been to reinforce the depleting population before it went extinct completely, or reintroduce the species if the extinction has actually happened, provided the habitat could still support the species. Although my thoughts on these issues had not yet taken a clear shape, I recommended the introduction of a male gaur from elsewhere, to improve the genetic vigor of the small, inbreeding Bandhavgarh population, at the time of my transfer out of the park in 1988. Whether that intervention would have saved the species from extinction or not, will never be known, but we are still fortunate to have brought the magnificent gaur back to Bandhavgarh, though after a complete wipe out, and at a much higher cost. Perhaps things were destined to be this way only, as we have no culture of actively managing wildlife.

Dream fulfilled

So, when I got into a position where I could push my vision of conservation, I started dreaming of bringing these lost species back to their native habitats and was fortunate to see some of these dreams turning into reality, before bidding farewell to my profession. Tiger was reintroduced in Panna Tiger Reserve in 2009, gaur (*Bos gaurus gaurus*) was reintroduced in Bandhavgarh Tiger Reserve in 2011 and supplemented again in 2012, and the blackbuck (*Antelope cervicapra*) was brought back to Kanha in 2011. Preparations for returning the *barasingha* (*Cervus duvauceli branderi*) to Satpura Tiger Reserve, 150 years after its last record in the area, were set in motion. I tried my best to fast track the introduction of lion and cheetah into the Kuno wildlife sanctuary which were on the active agenda of the Government of India. Before I demitted office, I made it a point to sow the seeds for the reintroduction of the white tiger in the Sanjay Dubri Tiger Reserve from where the last white was captured in 1951, in the hope that my successors might like to follow up. Without doubt, I was on cloud nine with excitement.

Although these projects needed a high level of technical knowledge, skill and commitment, the actual implementation of these projects was almost child's play in comparison with the struggles that went into making the decisions that allowed things to happen. While we may rue our lack of technical competence in doing conservation the way the rest of the world does, more than that we need to learn how to make conservation decisions quickly and correctly. This is the story of the travails that went into deciding that the reintroduction of gaur in Bandhavgarh Tiger Reserve was to be done and taking it to its logical conclusion. This is a commentary on the flawed systems and institutions that inhibit, rather than encourage, successful conservation in India.

The Bandhavgarh gaur

Gaur is found all over south, central and most of eastern India but its range has shrunk rapidly in the last century, mainly due to habitat loss. The central Indian population extended north up to Bandhavgarh and Sanjay national parks from where we lost it towards the end of the last century. Bandhavgarh is one of the most famous tiger reserves in the world. It had a small population of gaur, limited to some 20–30 animals. Though small, the population appeared to be stable till 1995, when it suddenly disappeared, except for one lone bull which lingered in the park till 1998. No clear reason for this extinction has been established so far. Successive managers must have tried, in their own ways, to figure out why this happened, but no clear pointers are available. Only some guesses can be made. The Bandhavgarh Gaur, like most gaur populations, had the habit of local seasonal migration. It used to be seen in the park only in winter and summer but disappeared at the beginning of the monsoon. It was generally believed that they migrated to the Ghunghuti area about 25 – 30 km south-east of the park. The park was enlarged, from 105 km² to 443 km², in 1984. I was the park director from July 1986 to July 1988. We started a year round wildlife monitoring programme, based on encounter records, in 1987, and the gaur herd was consistently recorded near Kallwah, even during monsoon. However, as we have very poor institutional memory, people continue to believe that the migration was not within the park but right up to Ghunghuti, although Ghunghuti forests were always known to have a resident population of their own.

Until recently there were two theories to explain the extinction. One was that they died due to some disease during the annual migration out of the park in 1995. The second was that their migration route was disrupted due to the construction of a thermal power station on their presumed migration route, at Pali, and something happened as a result of that. Although no carcasses were ever seen to suggest that, the disease theory was the more accepted hypothesis, till we hit upon another hypothesis in 2007.

While developing the project for reintroducing gaur back into Bandhavgarh, we naturally had to address the inevitable question as to why we lost the species from there in the first place. Till then, what we knew was only from hearsay, titbits from here and there. As several park managers had worked in the park during the relevant time, we thought each of them might have something to say about this episode, although none would have the whole picture. So, we called a meeting of all the directors and deputy directors of Bandhavgarh, some already retired, who had worked there in the nineties, to know from them what they had actually *seen*, rather than what they *thought* had happened to the gaur during those years.

While we all believed that the gaurs did not return to the park from their monsoon migration in 1995, Mr. O.P. Tiwari, who was the assistant director of Bandhavgarh in 1995, informed us that he found a record in his diary of seeing a herd of 13 gaurs close to the Tala gate on the day the park opened to tourists, i.e. the 1st of November 1995. This was quite startling, as this totally debunked the monsoon migration and disease theory. Mr. R.C. Sharma, who had returned as the park director in March 1996, informed us that he saw only a lone male in the park when he joined his new job. This bull lingered in the park till 1998. There is no record of how, where and when it died. So, it is clear that the bulk of the population disappeared sometime between November 1995 and March 1996. How it happened is still not known but there is scope for some new guesswork here. My guess is that this extinction was a mere accident, to which all small populations are vulnerable. Perhaps the entire population, consisting of just one herd, wandered out of the park to feed on crops, where it got scattered due to harassment from villagers and stray dogs, and the animals died their lonely deaths.

Failed translocations

The extinction of a large ungulate from a well-known protected area should have been a major event for the conservation world, but apart from casual conversations, the tragedy slipped from our radars quite quickly. Those who had seen the park prior to 1995 missed the gaur but perhaps the thought of reintroducing the species never crossed their minds because we did not have the competence to capture and translocate large ungulates. Some earlier attempts at translocating animals had miserably failed. In 1982, over a dozen barasinghas were captured in Kanha for translocation to Bandhavgarh, with the help of American veterinarians. One truck load was sent to Bandhavgarh but all were found dead on arrival. Others died in their crates in Kanha itself, while waiting for transportation. Some barasinghas were translocated from one part of Kanha to another, in several casual efforts, over many years, with very high mortality rates. Sporadic cases of gaur capture, over the years, had all resulted in deaths, earning it the title of a 'tender' species. An attempt to capture blackbucks in Karera sanctuary in 1995, by WII, again under American technical supervision, failed to capture a single animal. The successful translocation of rhino to Dudhwa national park, and the gharial in several north Indian rivers, seem like stories from another world and age.

A lucky coincidence changes the course of conservation in India

So the world had almost forgotten the Bandhavgarh gaur by 2005, when, strangely, seemingly unconnected events gave birth to the idea of bringing the species back. Almost about the time when I joined the office of the Chief Wildlife Warden of Madhya Pradesh as Additional Chief Wild Life Warden (in fact Additional Principal Chief Conservator of Forests), Conservation Corporation of Africa (now called "& Beyond"), a large wildlife tourism company which also manages private game reserves in Africa, decided to expand their operations into India. Sarath Champathi, the head naturalist at "Jungle Lodges and Resorts" (JLR), Karnataka, was selected by "& Beyond" as their head naturalist in India. When Sarath joined his new position with "& Beyond", which planned to set up four lodges in MP, and introduced his new company to me, particularly their expertise and experience in the capture and translocation of big game, I exhorted him to do something for wildlife in MP, to show that tourism can contribute to the conservation of wildlife. Borrowing an idea from the documentary 'Living with Tigers' made by John Varty, of Tiger Canyon fame, I suggested that "& Beyond" help us in the reintroduction of tigers into Madhav National Park, the way Varty had done. But Sarath wanted to do something in Bandhavgarh where his company was planning its first lodge. So the seed for bringing the gaur back to Bandhavgarh was sown. He reverted to me, after checking with his company, confirming that they would do whatever was required to help us reintroduce gaur in Bandhavgarh. In a few days, Les Carlisle, the inimitable Group Conservation Manager for the company, flew in to discuss the project. We met at my residence on a weekend. Les shared with me that he had been an 'animal catcher' all his life and had captured more than 40,000 heads of large game personally and that capturing and translocating a few gaurs was no big deal, in view of the expertise he could bring from South Africa. He assured me that his company would procure the services of other translocation experts, the best in South Africa, for guiding the operations on the ground, in addition to his own. I shared my apprehensions about the risk of high mortality, as experienced in an earlier case of aborted *barasingha* translocation to Bandhavgarh. Les assured me that the translocation technology had leapfrogged since then as customized drugs were available to minimize the risk of capture myopathy and other complications associated with the capture of animals. He told me stories of how he had transported rhinos and buffalos across continents and how they compose lion prides out of unrelated animals using long acting sedatives in confinement.

Government of India imposes impossible conditions

Convinced of their competence in the field and willingness to help us, I decided to try and build a consensus in the department for undertaking this novel operation. I could see the potential for this project to catapult India on to a totally new conservation trajectory. The Chief Wild Life Warden (CWLW), Dr. P. B. Gangopadhyay readily agreed. We developed a project to translocate 20 animals from Kanha to Bandhavgarh, as the earlier population had stayed stable around that number for a long time. Government of India, surprisingly, also issued its mandatory permission rather quickly, in September, 2007, "*subject to the pre-condition that a viable buffer zone would be created and the corridor connectivity would be restored. Further, the approval is subject to the following conditions:*

(a) Translocation process would be carried out in the presence of Wildlife officer(s) and trained veterinarian(s), and in accordance to the international norms & guidelines prescribed for this.

(b) Due care would be taken so as to cause minimum trauma to the animals while translocation.

(c) A representative of the Wildlife Institute of India, Dehradun, be present during the entire operation.

(d) A status report would be submitted to the Ministry."

(MoEF&CC Letter dated 19.09.2007).

As anybody can see, the four conditions are just silly, as all this was, in any case, going to be done. But the two *pre-conditions, i.e. creation of the buffer zone* and *the restoration of the corridor connectivity* (to where?) were deadly as they could never be fulfilled before implementing the project. Either these conditions were included unthinkingly, without understanding their implications, or they were deliberately included to kill the project. At that time I thought these conditions were only cosmetic, although they almost undid the project when tons of hard work and considerable money had already gone into it. We were just too happy to have the permission to go ahead, and plunged headlong into preparations!

While we were excited about the prospects of reversing the extinction of a large animal, and starting a new chapter in the annals of conservation in India, we had also started seeing the gaur translocation as a means of building the national capacity for undertaking similar ventures in the future. Therefore, we involved the WII in planning and executing the project, although the

GoI later made WII involvement a mandatory condition. WII conducted a Population and Habitat Viability Analysis (PHVA) of the species for Bandhavgarh and recommended that the minimum viable population size for Bandhavgarh would be 50 animals. WII also certified that the critical habitat conditions required for the species were available in the park and that the proposal satisfied all the conditions recommended by IUCN's guidelines for reintroduction of an endangered species.

Clouds start gathering

Although this was a path-breaking project, not everyone was happy with the idea. Several reports, some attributed to NTCA itself, criticizing the project as an unnecessary extravagance and a misplaced fancy, appeared in the press. Some said that the project was motivated by commercial interests because "& Beyond" was building a lodge in Bandhavgarh. Incidentally, some animals were seen in the forests nearly 25 km from the park, near Ghunghuti, in the summer of 2008. This fueled a spate of critical press reports saying that when the species was still present in the landscape, it was wasteful to spend money on bringing them into the park. Some worthies suggested that rather than picking animals for reintroduction from Kanha, we should lure the Ghunghuti herd into Bandhavgarh with the help of something like *mahua* (*Diospyros melanoxylon*) flowers. A meeting was called by the MoEF&CC, to discuss the project, at the behest of the NTCA on 17 September, 2008. The hostility to the project was palpable. Although the meeting was meant to discuss the gaur project, the deliberations were more about how the state had failed to protect the tigers in Panna. The basis of the opposition was what had already appeared in the press, mostly attributed to NTCA and an NGO called the Wildlife Protection Society of India (WPSI). WII had also informed Ministry for Environment and Forests (MOEF&CC), wrongly, that there was some "residual gaur population" in Bandhavgarh. I informed them that there were no gaur in Bandhavgarh and the few animals seen a few days ago were far from the park. In fact, there was no logical reason for NTCA to oppose the project except the petty egos of the officials. The benefits of the project to conservation were indisputable. The country was reversing the extinction of a magnificent species and was acquiring state-of-the-art conservation technology, without spending a penny from the government exchequer. Perhaps, the state's doing something creditable on its own was intolerable for NTCA officials and the other self-styled messiahs of conservation. NTCA had, by then, acquired more clout and resources than the MoEF&CC itself, of whose part it is, and had decided to show who the boss was. I pointed out the impossibility of the two principal 'preconditions' of the project and told them that the project was dead if they insisted on their compliance. It was obvious that MoEF&CC was looking for excuses to stall the project, under pressure from NTCA, but somehow was not able to summon enough courage to do so. At the end, it was agreed that I would "confirm the position about the residual population of gaur in Bandhavgarh National Park, along with an action plan for declaration of buffer zone and for corridor restoration/maintenance". We constituted an expert committee to prepare the proposals for the constitution of the buffer zones in the state, as required by the new law, and prepared a sham action plan costing Rs. 352.50 crore (3525 million) for the restoration of the imaginary corridor between Kanha and Bandhavgarh and reconfirmed that there were no gaurs in or near Bandhavgarh (letter dated 30th April 2009) and continued the preparations for implementing the project.

The death blow

Nothing happened for almost a year, till the D-day was announced. When everything was set, staff had been trained, equipment purchased, infrastructure built, the South Africans had even booked their tickets, the permission for capture was withdrawn by GoI, on the 3rd of February 2010, citing the alleged failure of the state to comply with the 'preconditions' imposed by MoEF&CC! By then, I had long been transferred to another position, in the wake of the Panna disaster, although the department had stayed committed to the project even in my absence.

Perhaps, the suspension of the permission was the result of a tactical error on the part of the CWLW. If he had just gone ahead and successfully translocated the animals, everything might have continued to be hunky dory. As ill luck would have it, just before the implementation of the project, scheduled for 18–28 February 2010, he wrote to Additional Director General (ADG) (Wildlife) and Member Secretary NTCA that all was set for the implementation of the project and invited them to be present on the site to provide "technical guidance" (letter dated 28th January, 2010). Perhaps this roused the sleeping hostility to the project in Delhi and they decided to strike before it was too late.

As the compliance with the preconditions was virtually impossible, I used to think that there was a tacit understanding between the Centre and the state, in the beginning, that a simple report showing the keenness of the state to comply with them would be enough. However, as time passed, the hostility to the project in Delhi grew, under pressure from NTCA and some Non-Governmental Organisations (NGOs) and self-serving activists, and the Crown decided to act just before the action was to start. The excuse used by GoI, to cancel the permission, was that neither the buffer zone for Bandhavgarh had been created nor the corridor connectivity between Kanha and Bandhavgarh had been restored. They knew that these utopian conditions were virtually impossible to comply with, because the creation of a buffer would require the consent of the unwilling people living in the proposed buffer, while the restoration of a wildlife corridor, passing through hundreds of villages and spread over thousands of square kilometres, was physically and financially a ludicrous idea. No wildlife corridor, over hundreds of miles, has ever been created where it does not already exist. We had submitted an action plan for reviving the corridor, but had never heard from them for nearly a year. However, in the cancellation letter, they said that they did not have the money to finance the corridor restoration work and that the state should use its own resources for this purpose. Till then, the translocation should be kept 'in abeyance'.

What the hell are MoEF&CC and NTCA doing here?

It may be quite intriguing to an outsider, or to a lay Indian, as to why a state needs the permission of the MOEF&CC for a simple management operation such as the translocation of a few animals within its boundaries. It is not a foreign policy or national security issue in which a consistency of approach is required between the states and the Centre. Nor are the bureaucrats, working for the Centre, who are all on short term deputation to the Centre from various states, in any way more competent than the state officials, in deciding what the states should or should not be doing. Selection for Central posts is never on the basis of the special qualifications of the candidates but only on the basis of seniority, even for specialized posts. For example, very few persons who have occupied the chair of the Director of Wildlife Preservation (ADG Wildlife), which is the highest statutory post under the WLPA since 1972, has ever managed a protected area himself, few have even been the CWLW of a state, perhaps with the singular exception of Mr. Sanjoy Debroy from Assam. Moreover, even if one has the field experience in one state, it in no way qualifies him or her to sit in judgment over the decisions or aspirations of other states, as the field conditions may vary drastically from state to state. For example, officers from the states where there is no forestry working (harvesting and regeneration of forests) or wildlife tourism, cannot be competent to pass judgment on these issues in other states. But because our law has empowered them to make decisions on a domain they hardly understand, these officers feel very insecure in making these decisions, and, as a result, often impose irrelevant and impossible conditions on the states, just to play safe.

So we had to take permission to translocate a few gaurs, because our law ordains it, from the officers at the Centre, who had never seen a gaur or its habitat in their lives. The WLPA treats 'capturing ... any wild animal ... and every attempt to do so' as *hunting,* and hunting (capture) of the species listed in schedule - I of the WLPA, for management purposes, can be done only with the prior permission of the GoI, as per section 12 of the Act. Any animal can be captured or killed by the order of the CWLW, if it becomes dangerous to human life, property, or crops, but, if the operation is for the purposes of education, scientific research or 'scientific management' the CWLW can issue such an order only with the prior permission of the state government or the central government, depending upon the schedule in which the species is listed. As gaur is listed in schedule - I of WLPA, the permission of the GoI was required in this case. Although the law empowers only the CWLW to prescribe the conditions under which the operation is to be carried out, GoI routinely imposes conditions of its own, as well. Generally, the conditions imposed by GoI are quite ridiculous and clearly show that these are being imposed only due to the insecurity and diffidence of the officers issuing the permission. The WLPA is replete with senseless provisions.

It is a war out there

Although I was not the CWLW when the permission was withdrawn, I was deeply upset, as a lot of *my* hard work and public money was going down the drain. More than that, the credibility of the state and its top brass, in the eyes of our foreign collaborators, was being destroyed. For a day or two, I thought it no longer mattered to me but soon I realized that it was *my* dream that was being ruined by a few incompetent officers in Delhi. I thought the state should go down fighting, even if it had to abandon the project. So I decided to make an attempt to save the project, despite it not being my mandate any more. I called the late Mr. Gangopadhyay, who had become the ADG (Forests) in Delhi by now, to share my anguish with him and discussed possible ways of saving the project. Naturally, I was expecting him to intervene in Delhi, but he was reluctant to enter the fray lest his interference beyond his jurisdiction may be resented by his colleagues. I was angry that the state was taking this nonsense from the Centre completely lying down as if the project did not matter to anybody. I wanted the state to take up the matter with the Centre at a higher level, but I could do nothing except drop polite hints, for fear of being seen as meddling. As nobody in the government had any personal stakes and commitment to the project, I knew that nothing would happen. Mr. Gangopadhyay, at first, did not like my idea of shaking up Delhi personally, again because I did not deal with the subject any longer, but, by the end of the conversation, he agreed that it might be the only way. He hinted that this might earn me the wrath of the powers that be, but I told him that I had nothing to lose. And my mind was made. While as CWLW my commitment to this project was because it was my job, now I acquired some kind of a missionary streak, which I never thought I had in me. I started thinking of a fight, with no holds barred. So, I shot off an angry letter (dated 08.02.2010, reproduced below) to Mr. M.B. Lall, the Additional Director General of Forests (Wildlife), hoping that he would realize his mistake.

"Dear Sh. Lall,

Although I am no longer the Chief Wildlife Warden of Madhya Pradesh, I am still constrained to express my deep anguish and disappointment at this move from the Government of India to block the above critical project, at the last minute. This diktat has not only resulted in wastage of millions of rupees spent on the project, after obtaining your permission to go ahead, and robbed the forest department and WII of a unique opportunity to acquire desperately required experience in mass translocation of large mammals, it has also destroyed the credibility of the state government, and several professionals, in the eyes of our national and international partners who have willingly agreed to contribute huge technical and financial resources to this path-breaking venture. I do not know if you are aware, our international collaborators, the Conservation Corporation of Africa (now renamed as '& Beyond') have provided on-the-job training, in South Africa, to three forest officers and two veterinarians from the MP Forest Department and WII, at their expense. They have donated darting equipment and drugs for the project while their Indian joint venture, The Taj Safaris Ltd, has donated two specially modified vehicles capable of transporting 12–16 large mammals in one go, never seen in India before. Not only this, '& Beyond' has also lined up 3–4 of world's best wildlife translocation experts to be present on the spot during the capture and translocation exercise, scheduled for 18th to 28th of February 2010, at no cost to us. The kind of expertise being placed at our disposal can be gauged from the fact that one of the experts involved, Mr. Les Carlisle, has captured and *transported more than 40,000 large mammals, all across the world. Others are equally or even more experienced. This project would have been one of the finest examples of Public Private Partnership (PPP) in conservation, anywhere in the world. Thanks to the continuous efforts of some elements in your ministry to murder this project, at the behest of some self-serving and self-seeking individuals outside, and your acquiescence to them, gaur may never come to Bandhavgarh now and we may have lost an opportunity, forever, to prevent several other extinctions, unless you reverse this decision immediately.*

Although your letter says that 'the translocation process may be kept in abeyance' till the so-called preconditions, namely, the creation of a buffer zone for Bandhavgarh Tiger Reserve and restoration of corridor connectivity between Kanha and Bandhavgarh, are complied with, you very well know that these are impossible conditions and the project will never go ahead if you insist on their compliance. As you very well know, the creation of a buffer zone, as per law, entirely depends on the consent of the local people to be part of the tiger reserve where they will have to suffer several restrictions due to our conservation laws, and has virtually nothing to do with the will of the State Government to create a buffer zone. We all know that no sane person will ever agree to live in a tiger reserve willingly.

As far as the restoration of the corridor is concerned, you yourself have mentioned that Government of India has no money for this purpose. I am sure you do not expect the State Government to be able to shell out a minimum of

Rs. 350 cr. for the purpose, although your letter, surprisingly, says so. By the way, nobody has ever resurrected a lost corridor in the world, as it requires relocation of huge human populations and requires unimaginable amounts of money to ensure compatibility of remaining communities with conservation, till eternity. We had presented a very modest plan to you and you do not have funds even for that.

So, the project is killed forever.

In any case, these two 'preconditions' have nothing to do with the chances of survival of the animals to be relocated. This species existed in Bandhavgarh National Park when the park was barely 105 km^2, while we lost it when the park was already 445 km^2 for over a decade. Adding a few more hectares, that too as a buffer zone, will be of no consequence. We discussed these issues threadbare in the meeting in your office and, I believe, we had a tacit understanding that you required only a plan, and would not insist on its complete implementation before moving the animals in.

Mr. Lall, I would humbly like to urge you that the role of the Ministry is not to put roadblocks in the way of conservation initiatives of the States. We expect its officials not to misuse the statutory powers vested in them to discourage the states from innovations and creativity, just to placate and glorify some vociferous lobbies outside the government, encouraged by some inside elements for their own benefit. Imposing conditions on such critical projects shows as if the State was a private business entity seeking favours from the Ministry. It is embarrassing for the State, to say the least, and shows the Centre and States almost in a superior-inferior relationship which the constitution never meant. You know I have been advocating radical changes in our laws, in favour of state level flexibility, primarily to prevent such whimsical attitudes of some individuals from further endangering our precious wildlife over the entire country.

May I mention here that we suffered the ignominy of losing all the tigers from Panna, partly, because the Ministry, especially NTCA, took over 7 months, to issue the permission, ridden with similar impossible conditions, to bring two tigresses from other parks to Panna? By then the few remaining tigers had also wandered out, most probably in search of females. We brought tigers to Panna in spite of the Ministry, not with its support.

When the State wanted to reintroduce tigers into Madhav National Park, under the advice of some of the finest wildlife experts of the country, including WII, your office blocked it by imposing the same conditions. Although one or two tigers have naturally moved into that park but they will perish if the population is not artificially reinforced. Obviously the Ministry would prefer to let these tigers die, without reproducing, rather than budge from its atrocious conditions.

It seems the Ministry is using the lack of corridors and buffers as convenient tools to kill other conservation initiatives in order to perpetuate the utopian prescriptions of some people in the Ministry who are far removed from ground realities. The current case is another example of the apathy of the Ministry to the plight of the shrinking, endangered, species. It seems it is interested more in paperwork to safeguard itself against possible criticism rather than in action on the ground.

Sir, our job is not just to count and report extinctions to the world. We are meant to take action before things reach such a pass. Let us be criticised for failed actions, rather than for inaction.

As you know, this project was conceived as a twin vehicle of learning modern wildlife management and bringing an endangered species back to a lost habitat, under the guidance of the then CWLW of Madhya Pradesh, Dr. P.B. Gangopadhyay, who is currently the other ADGF in the Ministry. If you had consulted him before taking such a devastating decision, I am sure he would have put things in proper perspective. I am sure he will be equally anguished at learning that years of his hard work have gone down the drain. Even WII would have advised you against such a decision.

Sir, I implore you, as Director Wildlife Preservation, the highest statutory authority responsible for preserving our wildlife, to reverse your decision at the earliest and let the project go ahead as planned. If we let this opportunity pass, it will be a monumental mistake and future generations will remember you as its principal architect, although I believe your hand has been forced.

I apologise for my impatient words.

(Dr. HS Pabla)"

I think I would have found it difficult to sleep after seeing such a letter from a colleague, but nothing stirred in Delhi. Even when I came across the concerned officers in Delhi in meetings, no mention of the letter was made. Government of M.P. also wrote to Secretary MoEF&CC on 06.03.2010, to reconsider their decision "in the long term interest of wildlife conservation", but the letter was not even acknowledged, as usual. So, totally frustrated, I decided to call on the Minister for Environment and Forests (MEF), who already knew of my festering differences with his ministry over several issues as CWLW, and solicit his intervention.

The minister comes to the rescue, again.

I met the MEF Mr. Jairam Ramesh, along with Dr. PB Gangopadhyay. We told the minister about the importance of the gaur project and how the ministry was mistreating it. It did not take him long to realize the folly of his ministry. He immediately called Mr. Lall and Dr. Rajesh Gopal telling them that he was going to revive the project, and asked me to stay overnight to carry the permission with me. He, smilingly, asked me what I could do for him, if he gave the go ahead for the gaur project. Delighted, I said, "I can give you my left arm." He laughed and said that my left or right arm would be of no use to him and that the state should notify the buffer zones for the state's tiger reserves. I told him that, although the buffer zones are going to make no difference to the future of tigers, and that I was not the state's CWLW, I would do whatever I could to see that this legal formality is completed.

Despite the Minister's keenness, the permission was not issued for several more months. However, the matter stayed on the MEF's agenda, as I kept sending him SMS's, off and on. Once, while on a visit to WII, he surprised me with a phone call, to find out what matters were pending with the ministry (I had returned as the CWLW by then). I mentioned the blocked translocation projects i.e. the Panna tiger translocation and Bandhavgarh gaur translocation. As mentioned in the last chapter, he brought Dr. Rajesh Gopal to Bhopal with him, on his next visit to the city a few days later, and must have directed him to meet me to resolve all the pending issues with Madhya Pradesh. Although the permission was to be issued by the ministry, not by the NTCA, Rajesh called all the shots in Delhi. Rajesh and I discussed several issues and the gaur project was one of them. Although neither the buffer zone had been notified, nor a penny had been spent on the so-called corridor connectivity, Rajesh and I agreed on some face-saving paperwork it would take him to revive the permission. As agreed, I sent another request to the ministry to revive the permission, with a promise to create the buffer zone and revive the corridor on 13th August, 2010 and reminded them of the personal promise of MEF, to me and the Chief Minister, on 5th October. Despite his well-known opposition to it, he issued the permission from his office itself "in view of the steps taken by the State for complying with the preconditions ...." on 6th October 2010, although the original permission, and the cancellation, had come from the MOEF&CC directly (as the law provides). But for minister's intervention, the gaur would never have seen Bandhavgarh again!

The stupid law, again.

It took so much effort and struggle to get just one permission for something which I thought was completely non-controversial. In fact, our law is so complicated that few people understand it well, which, sometimes, is good. In this case, nobody knew how many permissions we needed before capturing the gaur from Kanha. While we needed Central permission for the capture of wild animals for management purposes, (section 12), we also needed the permission of National Board for Wildlife for 'removal' of wild animals from a national park {section 35 (6)} for the 'improvement and better management of wild life'. Both section 12 and section 35 (6) were applicable in this case, as we were removing wild animals from a national park and for the purpose of 'scientific management'. We followed only section 12 of the Act, and it took us five tumultuous years to do a small job. One can imagine our plight if we had chosen to go the way section 35 (6) ordains. It says:

"No person shall ... remove any wild life ... from a national park ... except in accordance with a permit granted by the Chief Wild Life Warden, and no such permit shall be granted unless the State Government being satisfied in consultation with the National Board that such removal ... is necessary for the improvement and better management of wild life therein, authorizes the issue of such permit."

The National Board invariably wants to see the recommendations of the State Board for Wildlife before it entertains any subject for deliberations. Both these boards are usually stocked with bleeding-heart conservationists, with their limited world-view, and loathe to approve anything that challenges their conservative vision. Both the protected areas are now tiger reserves as well. Nothing can happen there without the tacit or express support of the NTCA. GoI/NTCA do not give any permission without getting the recommendations of the Wildlife Institute of India. Above all, the Supreme Court has also directed, through its order dated 14.02.2000 (IA 1220, 548 in WP 202/1995), that nothing can be removed from a sanctuary or national park without their permission. The Supreme Court sends all such cases to the Central Empowered Committee (CEC) for consideration before adjudicating on it. So, speaking legalistically, we could not have captured gaurs from Kanha without the permission of the Supreme Court, although the court order talks specifically about *removal of dead, diseased, dying or wind-fallen trees, drift wood and grasses, etc.* If we had chosen to approach all these institutions, boards and courts, we can easily presume that we could have achieved nothing. Fortunately, no one discovered that we were using a legal short-cut to be able to accomplish this task. I discretely avoided bringing this discrepancy to anybody's notice, not even to my colleagues, lest some non-believer, or the media, got wind of it and spoiled the show. Despite this craftiness, it took five years for a CWLW to do something which should have been routine in a sane society. Obviously, it would probably take a park manager five lifetimes to be able to accomplish something considered out of the ordinary, under the current legal and administrative framework. So much for our federal system of governance and administrative efficiency!

"& Beyond" and Taj Safaris open their hearts and pockets

While all this struggle to prepare the stage for action was going on, we had continued preparing for the actual task. The first target was to bring in

20 animals and, if all went well, apply for permission to get in another 30 next year. "& Beyond" flew three foresters and two veterinarians, including one vet from WII, and two of the Taj Safaris (the joint venture between the Taj Hotels and "& Beyond", that operated their Indian lodges) staffers to South Africa for hands-on training and exposure to game capture and translocation. The team spent two weeks in South Africa as guests of "& Beyond", participating in the capture of rhinos, buffalos and several other species. The team also developed a detailed capture and translocation protocol to be used in gaur operation, including an inventory of drugs, equipment, manpower requirements, specifications of vehicles to be used, size and specifications of *bomas* (South African expression for enclosures) and so on, under the guidance of some very experienced South African experts. By the time the decks were finally cleared for the operation, *bomas* had been constructed in Kanha as well as Bandhavgarh, a large TATA truck (LPT 1613 PC) had been customized for transporting the animals, as per the specifications provided by the South Africans. The drugs had been imported, local staff had been oriented and briefed, darting equipment had been procured, and the services of two additional experts, Dr. David Cooper and Jeff Cooke from KZN Wildlife, had been enlisted. Les Carlisle had already made nearly a dozen trips to India to supervise the construction of the bomas, customization of transportation vehicles and sundry preparations. All the cost of international travel of Indian and South African staff, two trucks (TATA 1613 and TATA 407) and a DistInject darting gun were born by "&Beyond" and their Indian joint venture, while the department bore the cost of constructing the two bomas. As

soon as the revised permission from NTCA arrived, 20th January 2011 was announced as the D-day for the operations to begin. But, a final check of the inventories, about a week before the D-day, revealed that a few important supporting drugs were missing. A whirlwind of correspondence and phone calls to regulators (drugs were narcotics) ensured that the South Africans had the drugs in their bags when they boarded the flights to India. To be able to get import permissions from the Drug Controller General, Narcotics Bureau, Commissioner Animal Husbandry (GoI), Director General Customs, Director General Civil Aviation etc. in less than a week, in an overly bureaucratic India, was nothing short of a miracle.

The week history was made

Finally, between 20th and 28th January 2011, conservation history was made as 19 animals were translocated from Kanha to Bandhavgarh. During these few days, we not only reversed, hopefully irreversibly, the extinction of a magnificent animal from a well-known wildlife reserve of India, but also paved the way for preventing and reversing many more extinctions in future. In all 22 animals were darted, out of which one died due to aspiration pneumonia, and two were revived without capture. One of the released animals was found to be a mother whose calf was too young to be captured safely, while the other seemed to be rather too old to breed in the new habitat. The first animal we darted barely survived death after toppling into a dry stream bed, the second animal died of aspiration pneumonia (asphyxiation due to inhalation of vomit) and another sinking animal was just saved by the vets' wits, all on the first day.

I had my heart in my mouth all day. I had lost my CWLW job once, when Panna lost all its tigers, and was very close to losing it again. Several times during the day I came close to ordering a halt to the operations but my timidity could not stay the hand of destiny!

This week converted several foresters from *poor man's policemen* into wildlife managers, and dilettante veterinarians into confident handlers of dangerous drugs and animals. We saw how Les Carlisle saved a sedated animal from imminent death after it fell into a dry *nullah* on its neck. Les jumped off an elephant, before we could blink our eyes, and straightened the crumpled animal to sit on its chest. We also saw how he brought down a dazed gaur when it was wandering about aimlessly, after receiving a dart. Les again saved a darted animal from certain death by holding its head above water, after it wandered into a waterhole after taking the dart. Dr. Dave Cooper saved a sinking cow with a quick jab of Butorphanol. Jeff Cooke lured five gaurs into the truck by inviting them to attack a white flag. We had all heard of Etorphine Hydrochloride (M-99) but never touched it as it was considered more dangerous than other options, while Dave and Jeff thought it a safe bet and had used it on thousands of ungulates. We were amazed at the level of sophistication developed by the South African veterinarians in the use of drugs, as a cocktail of sedatives and tranquilisers (etorphine, azaperone, hyaluronidase, haloperidol perphenazine) were used for customized results: some kicking in immediately and staying effective for three to six hours, while others took effect after 10 hours and kept the animal calm for 7–8 days in its new habitat. By the end of the operation, our vets and other officers were able to handle all the equipment and drugs expertly, so much so that the last batch of animals were captured and translocated entirely by our own crew while the South Africans enjoyed tiger photography in Bandhavgarh. Some veterinary myths, regarding the safety of these drugs, were debunked as four calves were born within six months of translocation, as their mothers were, apparently, pregnant when captured. Although the project was meant to teach us Indians the art and science of translocating big game, perhaps the South Africans also learnt a thing or two, particularly how our riding elephants carried the darting crew to the middle of the gaur herds, unbelievable to Africans, and how our noisy workforce could deliver a darted animal to a waiting transport truck, or *boma*, in less than 20 minutes! Incidentally, three of the translocated animals died, due to different reasons, in the following year, while two of the calves survived, to make the total population 18, when the second lot of 31 animals arrived next year.

Second phase narrowly escapes guillotine

Encouraged by the success of this operation, we applied for GoI permission to translocate another 31 animals to complete the minimum number, as advised by WII, to start a viable population. As our credentials had been established by now, the permission came rather quickly. GoI also permitted us to create a second population of a much endangered deer, the *barasingha* (swamp deer) in Satpura Tiger Reserve, through translocation from Kanha, and to reintroduce blackbuck in Kanha. 31 gaurs were translocated between February 28 and March 7 of 2012. One of these females delivered a calf the very next day after arrival, completing the number, 50, predicted by WII's modeling to be safe against extinction in near future. This phase narrowly escaped being scrapped in the wake of high mortality among translocated black buck, a major agricultural pest in many states, which were translocated from agricultural fields of Seoni to Kanha in November 2011. Although the translocation of blackbuck had been completed, the GoI, living up to their reputation of being imperious in their relations with states, cancelled the permission to translocate *barasingha* but, thankfully, spared the gaur project.

The species seems to have successfully established in the park, with regular births and deaths. Despite predation and natural deaths, some due to disease, the population has been growing steadily and the number, in April 2018, is conservatively estimated to be over 150. They have spread to the entire park and, as Deputy Ranger Namdeo, who had seen the native population here, says in the documentary (see below), "It seems like they never went away".

Turning the clock back

As this was a unique management operation we wanted to film it to use it as a training tool for future operations as well for public broadcasting. Quite a few wildlife film makers sent me messages that they would like to film the operations but we could allow only one, as several photographers jostling for vantage positions could have been a hindrance to the crew. While I was thinking of inviting tenders from prospective film makers, "& Beyond" proposed that they could film the operations through a renowned South African filmmaker and make it a commercial product which could be broadcast on public media, and that any commercial gains from the film could be shared by the two organizations. I readily agreed to this proposal, as it would have saved us the hassles of selecting a film maker, besides earnings. However, before the arrangement could be finalized, the media got wind of the proposal and twisted it into something like the sale of the sovereignty of the country to the South Africans. Interestingly, a gentleman, who had famously filed a public interest litigation to ban tourism in Indian tiger reserves, even alleged my vested interest in the project as my family had shares in the South African company, and an imaginary daughter of mine was employed in their Indian venture. While I assured the South Africans that I would be able to convince the government to approve such an arrangement, "& Beyond" did not want any media controversy and offered to surrender all commercial rights to the MP Forest Department. However, finally, they decided not to bring any South African crew as this could also fuel media misrepresentation. Instead, they hired an Indian cameraman to film the operations and handed over the raw footage to us for whatever we wanted to do with it. As a commercial film is much more than the technical images, we, later, tried to sell this footage, through a public tender, to a commercial filmmaker with offer of facilitating further filming, but did not succeed. However, the department has been able to produce a reasonable documentary from the available footage, and the sundry photography done by the crew involved in the operations. The film, titled "Turning the Clock Back: The Bandhavgarh Gaur" was made by Mr. Anil Yadav free of cost, and is now used as a training tool all over the country.

Advent of a new conservation culture in MP

This project has had a huge impact on the wildlife management culture of the state. The confidence, knowledge and experience gained by the department through this project has given rise to a totally new culture in the state. Translocation of wildlife, which was virtually unheard of until this project came, has become commonplace now. The barasingha has already been introduced in Satpura Tiger Reserve and Van Vihar Bhopal. Thousands of spotted deer have been translocated from Pench, Bandhavgarh and Van Vihar to Satpura, Sanjay, Ratapani, Ralamandal and Narsinghgarh sanctuaries. Kanha has moved several hundred deer from the densely populated ranges into Supkhar and Bhaisanghat ranges, to populate the sites of relocated villages. The department has also perfected the technique to capture crop raiding nilgai (*Bosephalus tragocamelus*), using horses and helicopters to drive them into a boma. All this with virtually no mortality. Many states are visiting MP to learn these techniques and copy the equipment designs. It is unlikely that any ungulate species will go extinct from anywhere in MP now as we can reinforce the populations in time. All thanks to the gaur translocation project.

Imagine, GoI and NTCA did everything they could to kill this project!

Trust the states, please!

That this project succeeded, despite the hostility of the GoI, conservationists and the media, is nothing short of a miracle. While the existence of tigers, elephants, rhinos and gaur, among so many people, is itself a miracle, we can perhaps reduce the need for miracles by creating systems that allow states to take pride in and responsibility for conserving their heritage. The role of the central government should be to support the states in their initiatives, rather than dictating terms. When the states can reserve thousands of square miles of their forests for wildlife, they should not be expected to beg for GoI's permission to do what they think is critical for saving their *own* wildlife. Many states are already regretting their earlier enthusiasm in notifying their forests as sanctuaries for wildlife because the control of these areas now entirely rests with the Centre and central institutions. If this feeling persists and gains strength, states might lose interest in conservation completely. Under the current legal regime, no field officer or state agency dares to think out of the box as they dread having to go begging for permissions from dozens of jealous men, who may neither have the competence to evaluate the proposals nor the commitment to conservation. I was lucky to be in the same office for six years so as to be able to pursue some of my dreams but not many are as lucky. For states to be effective partners in conservation, they must be encouraged to do what they think best for them, even make mistakes. And to be accountable to society, not to the mandarins in Delhi, who may know, and care, much less.

CHAPTER 5

Blackbuck: Cropland to Kanha

Gaur the harbinger of a new culture

As stated in previous chapters, I was not happy with the forest department just being a poor man's police. Policing, along with other significantly technical operations, is an integral part of conservation the world over. But wildlife management, as practiced in India, involves very little other than patrolling the forests. Although several species have disappeared even from protected areas, we have continued to define our wildlife management merely as an anti-poaching effort, along with digging the odd water hole. I used to wonder, in my younger days, why the police or the army could not do a better job of preserving our wildlife, if it meant only patrolling the forests to catch poachers of trees and animals. I had already been talking about the need for a holistic wildlife management policy, which involved managing animal populations and habitats as well, when I joined the wildlife wing of the department in 2005. So, I started thinking of doing a bit of what I had been preaching. My first idea was to reintroduce tigers in Madhav National Park, which had had a resident tiger population until the mid-sixties of the twentieth century. This idea was supported by a 'high powered committee' constituted by the government to examine the viability of the project. However, before we could get down to doing something on this front, we lost all tigers from Panna and the focus shifted to reconstructing the Panna tiger population rather than chasing any other maverick idea. Reintroduction of gaur in Bandhavgarh was another of my fancies which finally turned into reality in January 2011. Emboldened by these two landmark achievements, I started dreaming of several other reintroduction projects, two of which, blackbuck (*Antelope cervicapra*) in Kanha and *barasingha* (*Cervus duvauceli branderi*) in Bori were, surprisingly, quickly approved by the state and central government. These projects were scheduled to be implemented in the winter of 2011-12.

The translocation of 50 blackbucks to Kanha Tiger Reserve, from the croplands of Seoni district, was carried out in November 2011. Half of the animals died over a period of two months after translocation. This account is an attempt to record the lessons from this adventure, as, perhaps, nobody is likely to publish a research paper on this project because we always want to hide and bury our failures.

Blackbuck is by no means a rare or endangered species in India, although it is listed in schedule I of the Act. It is found in almost every state except a few exceptions in the northeast and the Himalayas. The species has been classified as an endangered species in India, not because of its low numbers or spread, which are still significantly large, but perhaps because the long-term threats to the species are insurmountable. With some exceptions, the species is found only in croplands where it is in serious conflict with the local people and, consequently, has no long term future in these environments. Therefore, it is necessary to keep some animals in protected areas as an insurance against their total extinction outside.

Blackbucks of Kanha

The species existed in the central meadows of Kanha National Park until the late nineties, though in small numbers. As per available data since 1953, the population kept fluctuating below 100 till it finally disappeared in 1999. The population size stayed at 32–33 throughout the eighties, before starting the final decline into extinction. The species was then believed to be a bit incongruous in the middle of the luxuriant *sal* (*Shorea robusta*) forests of the park, although small populations still occur, of course in the crop fields, in the adjoining districts of Mandla (Nainpur area), Dindori and Seoni etc. The principal reason for its extinction from the park is believed to be predation by jackals on fawns, although other predators were equally abundant in the area. Perhaps the transformation of their former habitat into luxuriant grasslands, as a result of the relocation of villages, also contributed significantly to their demise. Since the seventies, a few animals were also kept in the predator-proof enclosure built for the preservation of the *barasingha*. However, the species suffered rather heavy predation, even within the enclosure, from pythons and occasional forays from leopards. The last animal, a male, died of old age within this enclosure.

Blackbuck in the Central Meadows, surrounded by verdant *sal* forests, used to be an exquisite sight for tourists. With the loss of the species, the visitor experience in Kanha had declined to some extent. More significantly, extinction of a species, recognized as endangered by the law, from a famous protected area like Kanha, shows our conservation strategies in poor light, as PAs are meant to preserve all their biodiversity. I wanted to restore the old Kanha experience for visitors, preserved in old photographs showing spotted deer, blackbuck and *barasingha*s grazing side by side, and had a desire to leave behind as intact a world as I had inherited when I entered forest service. After the success of the Panna and Bandhavgarh reintroductions, it seemed within my grasp and I wanted to give it a good shot. Apart from these rather holy objectives behind this project, I was seeing it as the means for developing an in-house capacity, which we woefully lacked, for protecting the croplands inhabited by this species all over the state. Although Kanha did not have enough habitat for a viable and self-sustaining population of blackbuck, especially with the chances of heavy predation, it did not matter to me. I thought we could always sustain a small population through translocation from the crop fields. Even if the animals did not survive long in Kanha, due to predation pressure or other reasons, Kanha could be used as a sponge for soaking up crop raiding animals in the nearby districts, I thought.

Translocation plan

My first thoughts were about capturing the animals one by one through chemical immobilization, under the supervision of our South African friends, with which we had had good success in the case of gaur translocation. However, about the same time, we learnt of the success of the Andhra Pradesh (AP) forest department in removing thousands of blackbucks from croplands through an indigenous method of capturing them at night, under the leadership of one Mr. Thulsi Rao, who had trained with me during my stint on the WII faculty. We invited Mr. Rao to Bhopal to discuss his methodology and the prospects of our staff getting training with his crew. He made a detailed presentation on the methodology of capture and transportation, and how the technique was developed after years of experimentation, sanctioned and encouraged by the chief minister of the state himself. The method involved, as explained to us, the crew, with glowing headlamps and buzzers, approaching pre-identified herds (leks) of blackbuck on dark nights and just grabbing the transfixed and confused animals one by one. It looked as simple as that. We were told that the method had been evolved by the *chenchu* tribals over centuries and that the department had simply refined it by replacing their flaming torches with the battery powered headlamps, and adding a buzzer for better effect. We questioned him intensively over the extent of mortality but he denied having noticed any significant mortality, except during the experimental stages. And they never used any sedatives or tranquilisers. I thought we could improve upon this technique by sedating the animals during transportation to reduce the possibility of capture myopathy, by transporting them in crates placed in customized trucks which we had acquired by then. So I dumped my original idea of chemical capture and informed Mr. Les Calisle, from South Africa, who had already become our standing advisor on such technical matters, of these developments. He was surprised at the claims of such low mortality, particularly without the use of sedatives, but with his characteristic modesty he said that local communities have evolved indigenous techniques to solve their problems the world over. Thus, on the basis of the assurances given by Mr. Rao, and our conversations with other senior officers of AP forest department, and our plans to use sedatives for transportation, we proposed this methodology to the central government for permission to translocate 50 animals from the croplands of adjoining districts to Kanha, in the first tranche. Although I mentioned up to 10% expected mortality in the project, I was naively confident that we could pull it off without any major hitch, as we intended to do an improvement over a proven technique.

The plan was to send a group of our people to participate in the AP capture operations for training, and then ask some experienced tribals from AP to lead and supervise our capture operations. But the training could not happen in time. For whatever reasons, Mr. Thulsi Rao, who had, by now, been appointed as an advisor to the AP forest department, post retirement, offered to undertake the project on a turnkey basis, through his own crew. I was glad to hear that as I was always worried about how much of the traditional skills of the *chenchus* our staff would be able to absorb in a session or two of formal training. So, we invited Mr. Rao to Kanha to interact with our staff once more and see the conditions under which the operations were to be conducted. He made another presentation on the methodology and his experience of having translocated over 6000 animals without any significant mortality in AP and Maharashtra and convinced our staff that it could be done as easily in MP.

Perfect start

So the date for beginning operations was set for the 14th of November 2011. We had a very small window for the operation as it had to happen on dark nights after the kharif crops had been harvested. The capture team, consisting of 14 experienced tribal animal catchers, went straight into the capture operation on the day of their arrival itself, as the locations of the herds had already been surveyed by the local staff. On the first night itself, the animal catchers came back with 4 animals on their shoulders. They were put in crates which had been prepared for their transportation and were sent to Kanha about 150 km away. The animals were released in a 2-ha observation enclosure hurriedly carved out of the existing 50 ha *barasingha* enclosure. The capture team surveyed the field during day time and conducted nightly operations targeting the herds located during the day. Over the next week, 50 animals in all were captured and transported, the maximum catch being 11 in a single night. One animal died during the capture but was not autopsied. The captured animals included 10 adult males, 7 young/sub adult males, 13 adult females and 20 young/sub adult females. Although our plan was to take 12 – 15 adult males and the remaining young to adult females, it was difficult to keep control of such details as the capture was purely opportunistic and one learned of the age and sex of the captured animal only after it had already gone through the trauma of capture. The captured animals had a preponderance of young animals, some obviously not even weaned, primarily because it was easier to capture the young animals. Although some captured males were released, as we were getting too many males, the catchers were reluctant to release them because they were to be paid on the basis of the animals delivered.

The capture operations were halted, till the next day, as soon as the moon appeared. The transported animals were released into the main enclosure after it appeared that the smaller enclosure appeared to be too crowded. The animals in the enclosure seemed to be normal, except that some animals seemed a bit slow and disoriented. The capture team was accompanied by a local team of 14 staff members and labourers from Kanha, to learn the ropes, but they could hardly learn anything as it was difficult for them to keep up with the catchers in the night, as they scattered after the scattering herds. Although we were initially under the impression that the capture process did not involve any chase, and the curious animals, confused by the sound of an approaching buzzer and the light of the lamp, just allowed themselves to be grabbed easily, in fact the process involved a considerable amount of chase, after the animals realized what was in store. As the herd scattered, each of the catchers selected his quarry and chased it till it was overpowered and tied. It was virtually impossible for the local staff to keep pace with the chase at night. One wildlife veterinarian, Dr. AK Mishra, was on duty at the capture site throughout the operation. Other senior staff from Kanha took turns to observe the operations. An excited Dr. Mishra rang me, at about 9.00 pm on the first night, to say that four animals had been captured and were on their way to Kanha. I asked him what sedatives were given before transportation. He had given none, thinking that it was not advisable to interfere with a proven technique. After he found me worried, he called Dr. Parag Nigam, at WII who also, reportedly, agreed that it was not necessary to use sedatives on the animals, in the light of the experience of the AP team. The mission was completed on 21st November, with just one mortality. I was in Kanha, a day after the operation was completed and was extremely happy on seeing blackbucks in Kanha, again, after nearly 20 years. It seemed the sedatives would have been an unnecessary intrusion into a tried and tested technique. Alas it was not to be!

Shock after euphoria

We had not yet got over the euphoria of having achieved another landmark success in conservation, when, to my horror, on the 29th of November, a press reporter called me to find out whether I was aware of the death of 9 blackbucks in Kanha. I told him that I was not, and called Kanha to find out. The sad report was confirmed. The staff monitoring the released animals had seen three putrefied carcasses of young blackbucks in the grass on 24th November, and found another 6 on subsequent days. The enclosure had rather thick grass growth and it was difficult to trace dead bodies easily. On searching the enclosure intensively, we found another 7 carcasses. I reached Kanha to take stock of the situation on 30th November. All except one of the surviving animals seemed healthy, agile and alert, but we continued to recover dead bodies, sporadically, until 25th January. The total toll rose to 24, making it almost 50% of the captured animals. Although some of the carcasses were so rotten that their sex and age determination was difficult, looking at the surviving population it was obvious that most of the deaths were among the females, that too the younger ones. Out of a total stock of 17 males (10 adult and 7 immature) and 33 females (20 immature and 13 adult), dead bodies of 7 males (one adult and 6 immature) and 10 females (one adult and 9 immature) were classified while the remaining 7 other carcasses could not be aged or sexed because they were badly putrefied. The surviving stock consists of 11 males and 14 females, of all ages. All the post mortem reports confirmed capture myopathy as the cause of deaths. Les Carlisle and Dr. Dave Cooper, who had so ably assisted us in a near flawless gaur translocation, confirmed the conclusions based on their long experience. In simple terms, capture myopathy means necrosis (death) of muscular tissues resulting in heart attack or respiratory failure. It is a very complex condition and can result from physical or psychological stress during capture and transportation and may occur upto 3—4 weeks after the actual operation.

The Crown strikes back

The consequences of such large scale mortality were obviously going to be grave. Although we had already captured the permitted number, the Government of India cancelled our permission for any further translocations until further notice on 30th November 2011. The GoI also cancelled our permission for reintroduction of *barasingha* into Bori sanctuary, meant to be a hedge against the extinction of its only population in Kanha, vide the same letter. I was sadder about the loss of the opportunity for *barasingha* translocation, which was scheduled for the middle of January 2012, although the loss of face after such resounding successes in Panna and Bandhavgarh was also quite embarrassing. I pleaded with government of India not to cancel the *barasingha* permission, as all the preparations were in place, but they did not relent. Fortunately, they spared the second instalment of gaur translocation scheduled for March the same year.

As expected, media and our armchair experts started baying for blood, as soon as the news of the mortalities broke. Some compared the deaths to poaching of the species by well-known Bollywood stars. Some questioned the very need for translocation, while others questioned the wisdom of keeping the species in the same enclosure where a much more endangered species, the *barasingha* was housed. Government of MP ordered an enquiry into the press reports by a former Principal Secretary of the Forest Department. This report came in November 2012 but by then the temperatures had cooled down and everybody had forgotten the blackbucks. The findings were essentially what we had already concluded and reported to various authorities.

Could the mortality be averted?

Thus, I had to spend the last three months of my service defending the mistakes we had made in this operation. Although Thulsi Rao was untraceable for some time, I called my colleagues in AP to get their views on why we had so many deaths, they were as clueless as we were. The only difference between the practice in AP and our operation was that we released the animals in an observation enclosure while they released the animals in the open forest and there is no way of finding out what happens to the animals. Unless, of course, one really wants to know.

I think the most crucial mistake we made was our failure to differentiate between the objectives of their operations and ours. While we wanted to recreate a lost population, their objective was to remove animals from the croplands, ostensibly alive, but it did not matter much if many of them died.

Secondly, why the AP authorities did not admit to mortalities during the operation is very surprising, as, we found out later, by talking to the tribals who captured the animals, they did experience large scale mortality and injuries. While they neither knew, nor did they care, what happened to the animals after release, we learnt that AP experienced a lot of deaths and injuries during the operation itself, although we saw little mortality during capture. The reason is that their operation is much more crude and cruel, if I may say so, in that the captured animals have to wait, with their legs tied, and without any sedation, for hours, sometimes days, before they can be transported, over 400–500 km to the Nagarjunasagar Sriselam Tiger Reserve for release. The pain of being captured and tied is much worse, producing much more shock and vulnerability to capture myopathy. In contrast, we transported the animals in specially made crates, within minutes of capture and over a much shorter distance of about 150 km and still suffered huge post release mortality for nearly two months after release. While we were observing the animals in the enclosure, AP had no way of, nor perhaps any desire for, monitoring the fate of the released animals. So, we can safely presume that mortality in AP must have been much more than what we experienced. *Therefore, the lesson is that we should have examined the AP experience and methodology much more critically before taking their word for it.*

Secondly, we should have stuck to our original plan of sedating the animals before transportation to prevent shock. While in the case of our gaur translocation, we had used a combination of several sedatives and tranquilisers, such as etorphine hydrochloride, ketamine, perphenazine, haloparadol, butorphanol, azaperone, hyaluronidase etc. the vets decided not to use them on blackbucks. Obviously we all became quite complacent about the whole issue, because of the assurances given by the AP foresters and tribals. Despite the sedation being clearly a part of the methodology approved in the project, somehow, our vets did not prepare for using the drugs at all. In fact when I asked the vet on duty what sedative had he used, he seemed to be taken by surprise. Perhaps, using the drugs without enough homework on choice of drugs and doses, would have been an equally bad disaster. More than anybody else, the vets should have cautioned us against going into the operation without adequate preparations about drugs. We had a huge advantage over Andhra Pradesh forest department in that we had a bunch of experienced wildlife vets who had just completed a flawless gaur translocation. But, unfortunately, we did not use this strength at all, as our vets on duty were there as mere spectators, rather than being in charge of the operations. Perhaps, the difficulty in communications with the Telugu-speaking *chenchus* was another factor why the staff in charge could not convey their concerns regarding animal safety to them adequately.

Equally crucially, the operation also seems to have suffered from lack of senior level supervision. The legislative assembly was still in session, and the officers were busy dealing with assembly questions. None of my senior colleagues could be spared and the programme could also not be postponed, as this was the only window available. The senior officers from Kanha did visit the operations, but more as visitors rather than with the intention of controlling the operations. The primary reason why the animals were inflicted with myopathy was because the operation involved a considerable chase, sometimes running into one or two kilometres, and struggle during capture, while our impression was that this was going to be a very quiet operation. As we were taught, only a year ago, by Les Carlisle and co., that capture myopathy is the result of struggle during capture, and that it can come to light several weeks later, we should have halted the operations the moment we knew that it involved struggle by the animal, especially when no sedatives were being used. They could at least have prevented the capture of little calves who were not even weaned. Perhaps, if the senior officers had been involved in the operations, they would have been worried at the way the operation was being conducted, although it was equally possible that, because there were no immediate mortalities, they too would have let the operation continue. Of course we are being wiser with the advantage of hindsight.

Another factor that may have resulted in the mortality is the fact that the *chenchu* tribals involved in the capture were instinctive hunters who know only killing, not saving, a captured animal. Perhaps, if we had sensitized them to the issue of safety of the animals, they may have been more careful with them and some of the mortality could have been prevented.

We were complacent

Apart from these real shortcomings, we also committed some silly mistakes which government officials would often not do. That is about the paperwork. The GoI permission for translocation had come with certain conditions but perhaps in our exuberance after the success of tiger and gaur translocations, we completely forgot about these conditions. Even if everything had gone well, media would still have pointed out our delinquency, sooner or later. But now that we had botched the operation, there was the real danger of someone handing over a charge sheet to me or my field colleagues for non-compliance with mandatory conditions of the permission. The enquiry report did mention this issue in a passing way, but did not, fortunately, dwell too much on this issue. Just for the sake of record, the conditions imposed by GoI were as follows:

(a) Habitat viability analysis of relocation site be carried out before undertaking translocation of blackbucks.

(b) Appropriate methodology, as used earlier for translocation of blackbucks, would be used.

(c) Post translocation monitoring protocol along with a comprehensive action plan should be prepared in advance.

(d) The Wildlife Institute of India will also be consulted while making the action plan and its execution.

(e) It would be ensured that a veterinarian be present during the entire operation.

(f) It would be ensured that minimum trauma be caused to the animals during the operation.

(g) A detailed report on the translocation would be submitted to the Ministry and thereafter, the Ministry would consider grant of permission for the next batch of blackbucks, as appropriate.

Although we knew that GoI officials had included these conditions just to cover any risk to themselves, in case something went wrong, we should have created a compliance trail for each of them, as is customary in government. But, somehow, we forgot this cardinal rule. Although most of the conditions were complied with, without ever thinking about them, we completely forgot about the habitat viability analysis and, perhaps, inviting WII to participate. Although nobody made a big deal of it, I think it was a serious lapse on our part, even though the analysis would have been only an academic exercise. I had lost the CWLW's chair once, for no fault of mine, when Panna lost its tigers, but this time I would have had a tough time defending myself if someone wanted to take it out on me.

Post Script

The survivors of this operation have bred well in the enclosure and now number more than 50. Out of these, 30 animals have already been released into the Kanha meadows (by 2017). The population viability analysis conducted by WII had recommended a viable population of 100 animals. Therefore, these 30 animals are inadequate to create a viable population under the heavy predation pressure to which these animals are likely to be exposed. Therefore another translocation effort is required to create a viable population of at least 100 animals, before this chapter is closed. As the founding stock is coming from the wild and has not displayed any pest load, they may be hard released rather than putting them in the enclosure again,

Moreover, a keen eye has to be kept on the habitat requirement of the species. As Kanha meadows have a slightly taller mix of grasses for the liking of blackbuck, a suitable burning regime will have to be developed to keep some parts of the meadows suitable for the species. In fact the original plan was to release the species in Raunda meadow which has relatively low grasses, but the plan was changed at the last minute by the local authorities.

Conclusion

Although these deaths are lamentable, science and skills are founded as much on failures as on successes. If these animals had not died, perhaps we would have concluded that the South Africans make a bit too much of capture myopathy and even our *chenchus* know better than them. I had seen capture myopathy in my early career when several *barasinghas* died overnight in the transportation crates on the way to Bandhavgarh from Kanha in January 1982. I had also seen healthy *barasinghas* dying, seemingly inexplicably, 2–3 days after transportation from Kanha to Supkhar within the same park. But now we know that captured or translocated animals should be treated as safe only when several months have passed. As I am hoping that wildlife management in India, particularly in MP, is going to involve much more emphasis on moving animals around than at present (it has already happened), without this setback we would have entered that phase rather underprepared. Perhaps these deaths will save many lives in future, some of which may be much rarer and endangered than the bucks and does we lost. Although there is no justification for making avoidable mistakes, especially if they are fatal, it is a fact that every country has gone through the process of developing the capture techniques, for its endemic species, in the same way: they started with high rates of mortality and reduced these losses gradually to almost negligible levels. If these experiences are remembered by our future wildlife managers, these deaths will not be in vain.

Perhaps these lessons have *been* well learnt as the department has translocated thousands of spotted deer, barasinghas and blue bulls since then with virtually no mortality.

CHAPTER 6

Saving Wildlife Tourism

Wildlife tourism in the 20th century

I had chosen to be a wildlife manager, immediately after joining the IFS, because I was smitten by the natural beauty of Kanha National Park, what with all its deer and tigers. Out of the three national parks of Madhya Pradesh, of that time, i.e. Kanha, Madhav and Bandhavgarh (all others were notified later in 1981), I had seen only Kanha, which was nothing short of a paradise to me. From the moment I entered Kanha for the first time, I had started dreaming of spending a lifetime there. It had all the elements of a glamorous life for a forester, with magnificent forests full of tigers, rest houses in beautiful locations, opportunities for meeting important people almost every day and some strange sense of power to show tigers to the drooling public. Although management of tourism was the essence of life in Kanha, I too, like most others of my fraternity, used to say that tourism was a distraction in our principal job of maintaining a healthy forest and wildlife populations. Looking back, I think such statements were hollow, and perhaps dishonest, as, deep down, we knew that our recognition and importance was only because of tourism. Although now we think of wildlife tourism as a tool to save wildlife, back then we had no idea of the power of tourism and it was allowed merely as an obligatory service for the public. The park entry fee was only Rs. 2 per person and for almost 20 years it remained the same. Although many people were reluctant to pay even this princely sum, we often said, when asked why the tariff was so low, that tourism was not for making money. No jobs were linked with tourism as there were no private lodges (except the Kipling Camp), no private jeeps for hire, and no guides. Although, for the lay public, national parks were always meant to serve tourism, just as we did not fully comprehend why preserving marauding wild animals was important, we also did not know the real value of tourism to conservation, except having some vague sense of educating the public about conservation issues and igniting the love of the wild. Like everyone else, I too spent decades in the forest service dealing with the mundane routine, without giving these issues any deep thought. For me, ecological reasons and the beauty of wild animals, and of wild places, were reason enough to preserve wildlife. However, this was not enough for everyone, particularly in the face of the losses caused by wild animals and the spiralling need for more space for the growing human population and prosperity. Looking for a stronger and clinching justification for preserving wild animals, I started thinking that wildlife would have to compete with other land uses to earn active public support (not just sympathy). As wildlife could not be hunted and traded (although I have been arguing in favour of these), the only way wildlife could generate economic returns for human beings was through tourism. At that time, we thought of the value of tourism only in terms of park revenues, not in terms of the jobs it could create outside the parks. Thus, the only way tourism could become a significant conservation tool was if we could increase park revenues and share these with the neigbouring communities who, incidentally, suffered more if conservation was successful. So, towards the end of the nineties, I started talking of increasing tourism tariffs and traffic in the parks, for strengthening conservation, rather than just as a benevolent service to the society. And when I came into the wildlife wing in 2005, the value of tourism as a conservation and economic tool had already become a talking point and I became actively involved in promoting tourism in our parks. Madhya Pradesh had already allowed the parks to retain all their tourism revenues for local use, and we wanted to make these revenues significant in view of the perennial shortage of funds provided by the government for the maintenance of the parks.

Until the end of the century, wildlife tourism in our parks had remained virtually stagnant for nearly 25 years. The public was just not interested in visiting national parks, either due to lack of awareness or of means, perhaps both. Visits to national parks started looking glamorous by the nineties, due to the exposure unleashed by television. Perhaps in view of the crisis underlined by the Sariska debacle, people started flocking to the parks to see wild tigers while they were still around, which, they thought, might not be for long.

This gave a spur to our park revenues while scores of lodges started occupying the fringes of the parks, creating thousands of jobs in these remote areas. Rural infrastructure in these areas started improving for the convenience of visitors and, thus, the development of these forgotten areas also got a little fillip. Good or bad, the surrounds of some parks started looking like mini towns, especially at night. We started financing the protection of poorer sanctuaries, and started giving development grants to the neighbouring communities, out of the tourism revenues. We were able to keep our vehicles running, forest fires under check, and patrols moving, even when government grants were exhausted. We financed the reintroduction of tigers in Panna, gaur in Bandhavgarh, blackbuck in Kanha and *barasingha* in Satpura out of the revenues generated by tourism. Visits of world famous experts, to improve our management skills, were financed by the tourism revenues and, importantly, by tourism businesses. I even wrote a scheme (although it did not go anywhere as I retired about the same time) called "Tigers for People" aimed at providing universal health insurance to all the villages in the buffer zones of our parks, and scholarships for all the students going to professional colleges. We started taking some baby steps in diversifying and dispersing tourism in the parks in order to minimise overcrowding of sensitive habitats, and for improving visitor experience, and, of course, visitor footprint. I thought the chances of making conservation of wildlife sustainable were looking up.

Law on wildlife tourism

The Wild Life (Protection) Act, 1972 is a strange law. It provides that the nominal control and management of PAs, some of which are tiger reserves now, vests with the states, through the CWLW (section 33), but the power to approve the management plans (tiger conservation plans) of tiger reserves lies with the Centre, through the NTCA {section 38. O (a)}. Further, the states can allow tourism in PAs (section 27 and 28), including tiger reserves, but the Centre will lay down "normative standards" for such tourism. To cap it all, every "person, officer or authority" in the country is "bound to comply with" the directions of the NTCA {section 38.0 (2)}, which means a violation of any such direction is a violation of the law itself, inviting criminal proceedings against erring officials. A conviction in such a case can result in a *minimum* imprisonment of 7 years and a fine which may amount to anything from Rupees 5 lakh to 50 lakh. This law was passed without mandatory consultations with the states and the only explanation for having such a law can be that the central government thinks that the state governments are populated by morons incapable of deciding how their PAs and wildlife are to be managed!

NTCA bans tourism in core areas of tiger reserves

So, when all looked good and improving, NTCA was formed in 2006, through an amendment of the Wild Life (Protection) Act, 1972 and it started flexing its muscle immediately. Although Project Tiger directorate (which became NTCA) had been recommending a weird methodology for calculating tourism carrying capacity for many years, it had not issued any detailed guidelines for managing tourism in the reserves. However, its hand strengthened by the new law, NTCA started issuing repeated guidelines for constricting tourism in tiger reserves and other PAs. The first draft "Strategy for Ecotourism in Protected Areas", circulated for comments in December 2006 (January 2007), gave no inkling of what was going on in the minds of the mandarins in Delhi. It was a benign document, full of mostly inane statements. Then came the "REVISED GUIDELINES FOR THE ONGOING CENTRALLY SPONSORED SCHEME OF PROJECT TIGER" (February 2008), which mandated that *"The core/critical tiger habitats* (of tiger reserves) *would not be used for any form of tourism, and the ongoing tourism activities in such areas should be phased out in the fringe/buffer areas, without affecting its corridor value."* Until then, very few tiger reserves had buffer zones and tiger tourism was all in the core zones. Implementation of these guidelines would have meant not only loss of significant revenue to the well-known parks, but also loss of several thousand jobs around the country. How such a stupid diktat can be issued by a government which has the responsibility for running a federal country of more than a billion people is absolutely astounding! However, although it was an alarming prescription, nobody took it seriously, thinking, perhaps, that it would never be implemented.

"Wildlife Ecotourism Guidelines" issued (for states' comments) on the 10th of April 2008, which followed the above guidelines, said nothing about the ban or phasing out tourism from PAs. But this draft was immediately replaced with another, curiously titled "Revised draft guidelines for Forest and Wildlife Ecotourism" on the same date, which contained the same dangerous potion which was delivered in the form of the guidelines for implementing Project Tiger mentioned above. Among other things, it said that *"All tourism activities should be promoted and fostered in a specially delineated tourism zone outside the National Park/Wildlife Sanctuary/core or critical tiger habitat of a Tiger Reserve."*

Madhya Pradesh retorts

I am not sure how other states reacted to these guidelines, but we, in MP, were just livid, and strongly objected to them. Our comments on these guidelines, sent on the 2nd of June 2008, and again on the 4th of November 2010, are reproduced below. For the sake of brevity, I am not reproducing the guidelines here. The comments clearly indicate what is being commented on.

Quote:

1) **General:** *The objective or intent of this document is not clear. It does not look like a policy document as it does not say, except for one or two statements in the preamble, what NTCA or GOI would like to pursue or support in the name of ecotourism. It is also not a technical document as it does not deal with the 'how to' side of ecotourism, except the calculation of carrying capacity. As any guideline coming from a statutory authority is likely to be seen as a directive that must be enforced, it is proposed that such*

guidelines must be issued only in exceptional situations. This document, in this form, is unlikely to be of any help to the states in promoting or regulating ecotourism but may lead to litigations if people pick up controversial elements, of their choice, to pursue their own agendas and convictions.

2) **Title:** *The word 'ecotourism' encompasses visits to forests and wildlife areas; there is no need to use these words again. The title can be either Guidelines for Ecotourism or Guidelines for Nature Tourism.*

3) **Preamble:**

a) *The value of ecotourism should not be seen only in limited terms of generating public education and awareness regarding conservation issues. Although this is a very important aspect, the main value of ecotourism is its commercial power. Ecotourism must be promoted, if for nothing else, because it can generate significant earnings for conservation as well as for communities all around, and far and wide. Those who economically benefit from conservation, through tourism, will support conservation of natural resources even more than the people who become aware and conscious of the need for conservation by visiting these areas, because of their direct and higher stakes.*

b) *Although it is true that ecotourism is a legitimate part of conservation/forestry, the GoI has not yet formally recognized it as such, especially in the context of FCA. The preamble conveys the meaning as if it is already 'recognised' as such under FCA. This may be looked into.*

4) *The recommendation that tourism be phased out of national parks, sanctuaries and core areas of tiger reserves is neither realistic nor otherwise desirable. We believe that* **regulated and sustainable tourism** *is both the motivation as well as the means for better protection of wildlife and its habitat and this tool should never be abandoned. Moreover, we have no right to destroy the livelihoods of thousands of people and communities who have learnt to depend on tourism over the years. We have strong support for conservation of wildlife primarily because a significant and influential section of our society has seen and enjoyed the beauty of our national parks. We ought not to kill this constituency by banning access to these areas.*

5) **General Objectives**

a) *The livelihood opportunities to the local communities, as a result of tourism, are not limited to their involvement in 'service delivery' alone. Tourism leads to all round development of the economy through promotion of businesses, employment and demand for local products and properties.*

b) *The objective of ecotourism cannot be to 'underline the vital role of forest/wildlife ecotourism in sustainable development of natural resources', as stated in the second objective. The objective should be to use its economic potential for this purpose, as stated in the next line.*

6) **Regarding Section 6.2**

a) *Rather than banning all construction within two kilometres of park boundaries, and thus alienating the immediate neighbours by denying them commercial benefits, it is proposed that we should aim at controlling the density of development in these areas rather than aiming to stifle such activity completely. The concern for corridors is genuine but the way it is proposed to be taken care of may be counterproductive.*

b) *We strongly oppose the intention to forbid, or phase out, tourism in protected areas, for reasons explained before. Even the restrictions on land use changes outside the PAs, as proposed in the section, should be imposed very cautiously. The PAs should not be the reason for denying its neighbours the means of improving their economic status.*

c) *Section 6.2.6 intends to regulate construction activity even beyond the 2 km belt mentioned earlier. There is no justification for such restrictions, more so if these cannot be enforced. How far (outer limit) shall we go with these restrictions? These are site specific issues and should be left to the states to deal with. As all states are developing their proposals for declaring ecosensitive zones around protected areas, they will certainly take care of such issues.*

d) *We should not dictate what kind of institutions should operate ecotourism in PAs. There can be a diversity of institutions and structures based on the nature and composition of the local communities, competence of the management staff, local political climate etc. By dictating that only one arrangement is good for the whole of country, we may end up stifling local creativity. Our only concern must be that tourism must benefit the PAs as well as the local communities, irrespective of the institutions or approaches.*

7) **Section 6.3.1:** *As stated above, environmental guidelines for ecosensitive zones are being developed by the states. Therefore there is no need to provide similar guidelines elsewhere, as this may lead to confusion and conflict.*

8) **Sections 8 to 11** *are of very general nature and need not be a part of mandatory guidelines.*

9) **Appendix-1:** *This is also not required as these issues are site specific and no one model can be good for the entire country.*

a) **Appendix-2 (Model Calculation of Carrying Capacity):** *We have found that the method illustrated here is not sufficiently scientific and objective. The concept of rotation factor and most of the correction factors are arbitrary. Moreover, tourism in our PAs should not be limited to only the wildlife safaris on vehicles. We need to promote less intrusive and low impact tourism, such as hiking, trekking, bird watching, use of machans and hides etc., along with the traditional safari activity. The concept of carrying capacity must take into account the potential of these activities as well.*

b) *To sum up, it is proposed that there is no need to issue these guidelines; unless the NTCA or GoI wants to make a policy statement through them. And these policies should be developed through debate and consensus building rather than by issuing directives. The guidelines should primarily be promotional in nature and intent, and should not tend to curb the creativity of the states and field officers by creating a national straitjacket into which every situation must fit. (unquote).*

For some reason, but perhaps due to the opposition from states like MP, the next version of the guidelines dropped the idea of altogether banning tourism in core areas. This was the document purportedly drafted by the Sujit Banerjee Committee, although the committee disowned it (see some more discussion on this issue later). The draft put up for public comments on the ministry's website on the 2nd of June 2011, titled "GUIDELINES FOR ECOTOURISM IN AND AROUND PROTECTED AREAS" said that:

"Given that traditional tourism has been happening in national parks/sanctuaries, many of which now form part of core/critical tiger habitat or critical wildlife habitat, and also taking note of the need to implement the provisions of the Wildlife (Protection) Act, 1972, the following norms maybe be adhered to in the context of ecological-tourism activities, and included in the ecotourism plan of the Protected Area. For critical wildlife habitats of national parks/sanctuaries and for core/critical tiger habitats of tiger reserves;

(a) Larger than 500 sq.km, 20% of such areas may be permitted for regulated ecotourism access, subject to the condition that 30%

of the surrounding buffer/fringe area should be restored as a wildlife habitat in 5 years.

(b) Smaller than 500 sq.km, 15% of such areas may be permitted for regulated ecotourism access, subject to the condition that 20% of the surrounding buffer/fringe area should be restored as a wildlife habitat in 5 years." (section 2.2.4).

Although these guidelines were also very restrictive, the conservation and tourism fraternity could still live with them because the document did not ban wildlife tourism altogether. Madhya Pradesh again took exception to several provisions such as miniscule tourism zones, an arbitrary method of calculating carrying capacity, local conservation cess (because it is impractical) and no tourism if villages have been relocated from a core area etc. In conclusion, the state said that *"these guidelines are neither based on internationally accepted principles and practices of ecotourism, nor are they likely to confer any benefits on conservation and communities."*(Letter dated 29.06.2011 to ADG).

Although these guidelines were some relief, compared with their previous version, the relief did not last long. When a Public Interest Litigation (PIL) reached the Supreme Court (see ahead), GoI/NTCA shocked the country by submitting an entirely new version of the guidelines to the court on 9th July, 2012 and reverted to the abandoned "need to provide inviolate core and buffer areas" and "phasing out (tourism) from core/critical areas". However, these guidelines were again replaced, with only cosmetic changes, under public pressure, by the ones that currently rule the country, except that the concept of banning tourism from protected areas seems to have been finally abandoned (see ahead).

Although all versions of tourism guidelines began with extolling the role of tourism in conservation and community welfare, such as *"Tourism in the form of ecotourism has the potential to enhance public awareness, education, and wildlife conservation, while providing nature-compatible local livelihoods and greater incomes for a large number of people living around natural ecosystem which can help to contribute directly to the protection of wildlife or forest areas, while making the local community stakeholders and owners in the process."* they invariably ended up in a slew of proposals to curb and kill it.

NTCA loses the battle in the high court

Although we were steadfastly opposing these regressive guidelines, all along we were worried that we might end up facing public interest litigations (PILs) from some publicity-mongering activists (as mentioned in our comments on draft guidelines, reproduced above), demanding implementation of the ban on tourism in core areas of tiger reserves. These fears came true when a PIL was filed in the High Court of MP asking the court to enforce the ban on wildlife tourism as proposed in the NTCA's guidelines on Project Tiger (WRIT PETITION NO. 12351/2010: AJAY DUBEY VS. NATIONAL TIGER CONSERVATION AUTHORITY AND OTHERS). The petition also prayed for an immediate stay on wildlife tourism, pending the final decision of the court. When we received the notice, I called member secretary of NTCA to request that we should not be taking opposing stands in the court and should discuss our responses before filing in the court. However, NTCA filed its response in the court, without trying to understand the state's dilemma, and supported the petitioner's prayer for banning wildlife tourism in the country. NTCA/GoI return stated that "core or critical tiger habitat areas of National Parks and Sanctuaries ... are required to be kept inviolate" and that "inviolate means free from disturbance by human beings". The return asserted that the Project Tiger Guidelines provided that *"The core/critical tiger habitats would not be used for any form of tourism, and the ongoing tourism activities in such areas should be phased out in the fringe/buffer areas, without affecting its corridor value."* This was done despite the fact that NTCA had already abandoned the idea of completely forbidding tourism in core areas of tiger reserves, as reflected in the later drafts of their guidelines on ecotourism in and around protected areas. The Minister for Environment and Forests, Mr. Jairam Ramesh had already issued a press statement on the 5th of May 2010, saying that "My attention has been drawn to some news reports that the Ministry of Environment and Forests is planning a ban on tourism in tiger reserves. I would like to state categorically that there is no such proposal." Although the idea of phasing out tourism was still embedded in the Project Tiger Guidelines for the management of tiger reserves, issued in February 2008, NTCA could have informed the court that they had been having second thoughts on the issue. Instead, NTCA jumped at the opportunity and, in contradiction to the position of GoI declared by the Minister, argued in the court that the provision to keep the core areas of tiger reserves "inviolate" {section 38V (4) of WLPA} implied a prohibition on tourism.

The state, while extolling the value of tourism to conservation and communities, strongly opposed this contention, and contested the notion that NTCA was the sole arbiter of tourism issues in protected areas, in view of the powers of the CWLW under section 28 and 33 of the Act. Thus, despite NTCA's support to the petition, the court refused to "prohibit tourism activities within the core/critical areas of tiger reserves in the State of Madhya Pradesh" because the expression "inviolate" only means "unhurt", "uninjured" "unpolluted" "unbroken" and does not imply a ban on tourism (order dated 19.01.2011). The court also said that the Project Tiger Guidelines provide for only phasing out of tourism from protected areas, not an immediate ban.

Although the application had many other prayers, such as a ban on mining in core areas, obliging the states to notify core and buffer zones of tiger reserves (most of which had already been notified), preparation of tiger conservation plans, implementations of tripartite MoUs (another illogical invention of NTCA) etc. everything else was forgotten in the fight to ban or save wildlife tourism.

When the case came up in the court, it was natural for me, as the CWLW of the state, to inform all stakeholders of the implications of the case for banning wildlife tourism and invite them to join forces with the state to ensure that it did not succeed. Interestingly, this message was publicised as a sign of some vested interest I had in protecting wildlife tourism. Some press reports alleged that I had shares in some tourism businesses. One report even alleged that an imaginary daughter of mine was working for "& Beyond", the South African partners of the Tatas, in their ecotourism business! The applicant, Mr. Ajay Dubey, used this simple message as a means to garner further publicity by asking for police security as I had asked the stakeholders "to take whatever steps you think will be appropriate to protect your interest". In fact, he continued to benefit from this *threat* long after I had retired from government service!

Drama in the Supreme Court

On the refusal of the High Court to grant an interim stay, the petitioner approached the Supreme Court (Special leave petition (civil) no.21339 of 2011) as if heavens would have fallen if he had had to wait till the final disposal of the case. Despite knowing fully well that NTCA was unlikely to budge from its course, we continued to make efforts to avoid another collision with the Centre in the Supreme Court. The chief secretary of Madhya Pradesh, Mr. Avani Vaish, requested the secretary MoEF&CC, Dr. Tishya Chatterjee (his batch mate) to intervene in the matter. He followed up his call with a telling letter dated 1st November, 2011 which went as follows:

"Dear Chatty,

As discussed over the phone, Government of India appears to be supporting a PIL No. 21339/2011 (Ajay Dube vs. NTCA and others) in the Supreme Court, seeking a ban on tourism in national parks, wildlife sanctuaries and tiger reserves. This is very surprising in view of the declaration made by the then Minister for Environment and Forests, in the Ministry's official press release dated 5th May 2010, that Government of India did not want to prohibit tourism in protected areas but, instead, it only wants to regulate it. Next hearing in the Supreme Court is on 9th November, 2011.

I hope you would agree that tourism is the principal driver of wildlife conservation all over the world and if India forbids tourism in protected areas, thousands of businesses will go bankrupt while millions of people will lose their livelihoods. It is an established fact that the presence of visitors in protected areas lends additional security to wildlife and its habitat. In MP, all the revenue earned by our protected areas is spent in strengthening their management and helping the local communities.

The impact of loss of livelihoods if tourism is banned in these areas will be very significant. If local communities around these protected areas lose their livelihoods (in addition to the use of natural resources which they have already lost), the result will be destruction of the habitat through illicit felling, grazing, poaching. I have no doubt that these communities will begin to see the protected areas as an enemy and not as a provider of income and livelihood.

We have informed Government of India and NTCA several times that we are not in favour of stopping tourism in protected areas, although the extent and nature of tourism can always be discussed. In any case, it is embarrassing if the states and the centre take contradictory stands in courts on matters of extreme public interest.

I would, therefore, request you to kindly reconsider the stand of your ministry in the current case so that we are able to jointly protect the interests of wildlife and communities dependent on wildlife tourism. Immediate action in this regard is requested in view of the impending hearing in the court."

I am not sure whether this letter was answered, or even acknowledged (perhaps not). However, there was no change in the stand of the GoI/NTCA in the court. How the ministry can go against the declared position of its minister will always be a mystery to anyone who knows, even remotely, the way the government works. NTCA officials had already declared their intention to outlaw wildlife tourism many times, God knows why, as they never gave any reasons. That the minister and the ministry allowed them to pursue their goal, in contradiction to the declared stand of the ministry, goes to show that most of the officials occupying big chairs were just dumb

Committee report fudged by NTCA

In response to the court order (dated 3rd April, 2012), GoI/NTCA submitted the draft guidelines for the regulation of tourism in tiger reserves in which they again committed to phase out tourism from core areas. The "Guidelines for Ecotourism in and around Protected Areas" submitted to the court on the 9th of July, 2012, provided, among other things:

"2.2.4: There is a need to adhere to the amended provisions of the Wildlife Protection Act

(1972) in terms of core/critical tiger habitat or critical wildlife habitat which have defined the need to provide inviolate core and buffer areas (designed for coexistence) in tiger reserves. Given that tourism has been happening in these core/critical areas, there is a need for phasing out and moving it to peripheral/buffer areas to benefit local communities. As an interim measure, the following norms may be adhered to in the context of community based ecotourism, and included in the ecotourism plan of the Protected Area.

> *(a) Larger than 500 sq.km of core/critical tiger habitat or critical wildlife habitat, a maximum of 20% (not exceeding the present practice) of such areas may be permitted for regulated community-based ecotourism access subject to the condition that 30% of the surrounding buffer/fringe area should be restored as a wildlife habitat in 5 years.*
>
> *(b) Smaller than 500 sq.km, a maximum of 10% (not exceeding the present practice) of such areas may be permitted for regulated ecotourism access, subject to the condition that 20% of the surrounding buffer/fringe area should be restored as a wildlife habitat in 5 years."*

The interesting thing is that these guidelines are claimed in the affidavit to have been prepared by a committee headed by Mr. Sujit Banerjee, former Secretary Tourism, GoI. The said committee submitted its report on the 30th of June 2011, while another draft, claimed to have been prepared by this committee, had already been circulated to the states for comments, and was also placed on the ministry's website for public comments on the 2nd of June 2011. Mr. Banerjee and other members of the committee took strong exception to this misdemeanour. Mr. Bittu Sahgal, a member of the committee, wrote to the Minister about the draft put up for public comments: "*As a member of the Committee I was rather taken aback to see several inclusions and deletions, which had the effect of negating the purpose and the very positive spirit of our many deliberations. ... In its present form the draft* (put up on the Ministry's website for public comments) *works directly against the letter and spirit of key points that had been agreed upon by the Chairman and other members.*"

To top it all, the draft submitted to the Supreme Court (mentioned above) was an entirely different one. Neither the draft submitted by the committee, nor the one put up for public comments, had the provision for phasing out tourism from PAs which mysteriously appeared in the draft submitted to the court! Significantly, the NTCA officials had inserted all their pet ideas in the committee's draft, when it was sent to them (to NTCA) for pre-review. The committee rejected these insertions in its final draft but NTCA submitted their own version to the court, pretending it to be the committee's recommendations.

The court, without going into the merits of the case, ordered that "*We make it clear that till the final directions issued by this Court with reference to the guidelines submitted by the National Tiger Conservation Authority of India, core zone or the core areas in the Tiger Reserved (sic) Areas will not be used for tourism"* (order dated 24th July 2012). In fact, the judges were annoyed at the inability of many states to notify mandatory buffer zones for tiger reserves, but their anger found its way into the tourism issue.

Political opposition to the ban

There was a widespread hue and cry against the stay and the draft guidelines, as expected. Many delegations met the Minister for Environment and Forests. Newspapers and television channels were full of stories and discussions about the case. Nowhere in these stories/discussions was there even an iota of support for the ban. The Chief Minister of Madhya Pradesh termed this decision "wrong and impractical". He met the Prime Minister on the 11th of August and requested GoI to come forward to pursue the case (for vacating the stay). The letter written by the Chief Minister to the Minister for Environment and Forests of GoI, on 30 July 2011, goes as follows:

"I wish to draw your kind attention to a matter of grave and immediate public interest arising from the interim ban on wildlife tourism in the core areas of Tiger Reserves. You would appreciate that conservation of wildlife, including in areas notified as tiger reserves, national parks and wildlife sanctuaries is inextricably linked to the welfare of local populations and their livelihoods. ... You will further appreciate that tourism ... has played a crucial role in enhancing the awareness of the urban population of the country to the need to protect wildlife. Another important outcome has been the beneficial impact this has had on

generation of livelihoods, overwhelmingly for the local population.

2. *In spite of the globally accepted role of ecotourism in conservation, the National Tiger Conservation Authority (NTCA) has been urging the states to 'phase out' tourism from these protected areas. We have conveyed our strong opposition to such a measure several times but the NTCA has not changed its directives.*

3. *Basing his premise on these directives, a public interest litigation (PIL) was filed in the High Court of Madhya Pradesh in 2010 demanding an immediate ban on tourism in the core areas of tiger reserves. On rejection by the High Court, the petitioner filed an SLP in the Supreme Court (21339/2011, Ajay Dubey VS NTCA and Ors.). I understand that MoEF&CC and NTCA, rather than opposing it, have supported the petition. The Supreme Court in its interim order dated 24th July, 2012 has banned all tourism in the core areas of tiger reserves, which will render hundreds of thousands of people jobless all across the country. Madhya Pradesh as the premier forest and wildlife state of the country will suffer the most. The ban will kill livelihoods and very severely impact tourism.*

4. *I fear that this development is likely to expose our forests and wildlife to the wrath*

of the people who lose jobs and whose businesses become loss-making propositions. This can only increase the threat to wildlife and forests in protected areas, giving rise to grave law and order situations. Vast tracts of well-endowed forest cannot be protected merely through policing by the forest department. ... Let us also not forget that in and around many of these wildlife habitats left wing extremism has also raised its ugly head.

5. *It is, therefore, my most fervent plea that the MoEF&CC and NTCA review their stand in the court to prevent what can lead to irreparable damage to the forest ecosystem and the local economies. The case is coming up for final arguments on 22nd August, 2012. It is important that immediate steps are taken by the concerned agencies. You may also like to review, in the long term interest of the country, the sweeping powers given to the central agencies, under the Wildlife (Protection) Act, 1972, which severely limits the creativity of the states for managing natural resources, while disregarding the need to strengthen their autonomy in the matter."*

An article in the Indian Express, written by Mr. Digvijay Singh, a prominent politician of the country, belonging to the party in power in Delhi, and a former Chief Minister of Madhya Pradesh, shows the depth of the anguish felt by the people over the issue.

"Ban on tourists, free run for poachers

The Indian Express | 2012 Aug 29.

I have been an avid wild-lifer from childhood and now, in politics, the only solace that I derive is when I am in a wildlife park. The Supreme Court ban on wildlife tourism in "core areas" has come as a shock to me.

With this ban on wildlife tourism, I would be denied, along with millions of wildlife enthusiasts, seeing the tiger in the forest.

Kaziranga, Kanha, Bandhavgarh, Ranthambore, Pench, Bandipur, Corbett, Gir and now Tadoba, are the most popular parks for wildlife tourism in the country. The tiger census has proved that the tiger population in these most-visited parks has gone up by over 25 per cent.

Take the examples of Sariska and Ranthambore, as both have a similar terrain. In Ranthambore, very popular with tourists, the tiger population went up, while in Sariska the poachers had a field day, sometimes with the connivance of forest officials, resulting in the tiger population being reduced to zero.

All the above mentioned parks are core areas and some of them, which have buffer areas, do not have wildlife. Most of the buffer areas have villages and mining factories and would take years to develop. It is also not easy to shift villages.

The Wildlife Institute of India, Dehradun, had conducted a study that shows tourism does not have a negative impact on tiger reserves or protected areas. This study, conducted between January and April 2011, was carried out in Pench National Park.

Environment and forests being on the Concurrent List of the Constitution, the power rests with the states who were not part of the consultation process while drafting these guidelines. All land of protected areas and national parks belong to the states, not to the government of India.

The guidelines for ecotourism in India, first submitted by the Union ministry of environment and forests to the Supreme Court, have not been approved, nor discussed by the National Board for Wildlife. Neither was it approved by the entire body of the National Tiger Conservation Authority (NTCA).

According to the Indian Wildlife (Protection) Act, the powers to allow/disallow tourism in parks rests with the chief wildlife warden of the state concerned.

The NTCA, in paragraph 2 of the guidelines, asks states to amend their laws accordingly to incorporate these guidelines. Guidelines cannot take away the constitutional rights of the state in the federal structure. They cannot, also, overrule the provisions of the wildlife act passed by Parliament. ....

Would the Supreme Court like to order against the provisions of the Wildlife Act and encroach upon the fundamental rights of the state government, guided simply by the whimsical, illogical and dictatorial guidelines drafted by a few people without the widest consultation with the stakeholders?

These guidelines directly affect the employment of over two lakh people and the livelihood of over one million, besides various other stakeholders in and around the 650 protected areas in our country. The majority of the employees in this sector are from the local communities, including tribals, and many who have been displaced from their original homes while creating these very national parks.

Ecotourism is the only sustainable, non-consumptive industry available to communities inhabiting the surroundings of our protected areas. Ecotourism can lower the cost of conservation that is borne primarily by these communities.

I saw a tribal youth, whose livelihood depended on tourism in Kanha, telling a news channel that if his livelihood is taken away, he would have no option but to cut the forest trees and kill tigers or become a Naxalite.

Take the case of African wildlife tourism, which is a significant part of the GDP of many African countries. Empirical evidence is available to prove that the critically endangered gorillas of Rwanda were saved only because of the positive impact of tourism on local economies.

I am appalled by the reaction of the Union tourism ministry which is blissfully unaware of the impact of these guidelines on the Indian tourism industry.

I am told that the author of these guidelines is Rajesh Gopal of the NTCA whom I have known since 1992 as the director of the Kanha National Park and who continued to stay there for the longest period. He has spent days with me when I was chief minister, and he took me around Kanha and was instrumental in my passion for wildlife photography, discussing how we could promote tourism in Kanha. I strongly recommended his name for director, Project Tiger, a position which he has continued to hold for the last 10 years, unheard of for a state cadre officer. I have the highest regard for his love of wildlife but I don't have a clue as to why he has authored a guideline which would not only finish wildlife tourism but also wildlife and forests in the core areas of our national parks.

The absence of a vigilant tourism industry, which has a vested interest in the conservation of wildlife and forests, would lead to what happened in Sariska. Poachers, with the connivance of lower officials, will have a field day once tourism stops.

I am sure this is not the objective of the MoEF&CC, the NTCA and the Supreme Court. I strongly plead with folded hands to the Supreme

Court and the MoEF&CC to reconsider their total ban on wildlife tourism."

Source:http://www.digvijayasingh.in/ban-on-tourists.html

NTCA buckles under public pressure

The comments of the states on the draft guidelines, submitted directly to the court, left no doubt about where the states stood on this issue. The response of Madhya Pradesh clearly said, among other things, that they "completely disagree" with the proposal to stop tourism because "it goes against the fundamental principles of these guidelines". Other states must have averred on the same lines.

This pressure, finally, forced NTCA to change its stand in the court. The court was informed on the next hearing (17th August, 2012) that the states were opposed to these guidelines as (the states believe) *"many people depend on tourism for their livelihood and ... stoppage of tourism may be a threat to wildlife and forests ... and common citizens would be deprived of an opportunity to appreciate our natural heritage"*. NTCA sought the permission of the court to hold further consultations. The guidelines now in force are the result of this *volte face* of the NTCA/GoI. The new guidelines were then drafted by another committee, which had no chairperson. Why NTCA/GOI continued to change the committees for drafting the same guidelines (Sunita Narain committee, Sujit Banerji Committee and then the one without any chair) is surprising and, perhaps, indicates a search for convenient minds.

The case had reached the Supreme Court as an appeal against the refusal by the High Court to stay tourism in PAs. The Supreme Court, after a short stay, allowed tourism to continue in accordance with the guidelines issued by NTCA/GoI but no discussion ever took place in the court on the merits and demerits of wildlife tourism. The High Court disposed of the main writ petition on 7th November 2012 on the ground that the Supreme Court was seized of the matter. The Supreme Court also disposed of the case on 29th March 2016, without any discussion on the core issue, saying that the case had come to them with the limited challenge against the interim order of the High Court, refusing to restrain tourism activities in the "core and critical areas" of tiger reserves and that "the petitioner shall be free to have Writ Petition No. 12352 of 2010 restored before the High Court for any further direction that he may seek". Thus, we may witness more drama when hearings in the High Court resume, if the application is restored.

The Supreme Court rescinded its interim stay in October 2012, just when the tourist season was about to start. As soon as the stay was withdrawn, everybody went home as if the case had been finally disposed by the court. The court order said that *"All the concerned authorities will ensure that the requirements in the aforesaid Guidelines for Tourism in and around the Tiger Reserves are complied with* **before** *tourism activities recommence"*, and that *"— we have not declared the Notification dated 15th October, 2012 either intra vires or ultra vires and ... it will be open to the aggrieved party to challenge the same before the appropriate forum"*. But no authority cared to check whether all the requirements of the guidelines had been complied with before recommencing tourism in the parks. As NTCA had to backtrack on its persistent stand on wildlife tourism under public pressure, it resigned to the collapse of its cherished dream and did not do any nit-picking about compliance with its guidelines. Although the guidelines still have several undesirable elements, some of which can never be complied with, nobody has ever challenged them in any forum and all seems quiet, until someone raises their hackles again.

Irrational tourism guidelines

The genesis of the writ petition in the High Court and the subsequent Special Leave Petition was the presence of the provision, to ban tourism in the core areas of tiger reserves, in the "REVISED GUIDELINES FOR THE ONGOING CENTRALLY SPONSORED SCHEME OF PROJECT TIGER" (February 2008). There were no specific Central guidelines on wildlife tourism at that time, although some drafts were under discussion. The extant "GUIDELINES FOR TOURISM IN AND AROUND TIGER RESERVES" have been issued as a part of the "Comprehensive Guidelines for Tiger Conservation and Tourism" in which the earlier provision to ban tourism in tiger reserves has also been deleted. The tourism guidelines, embedded in the comprehensive guidelines, are almost entirely the same as the draft submitted to the Court in July 2012, which attracted so much public anger, except that the provision to stop tourism after 5 years has been dropped and the limit on the tourism zones has been made uniform at 20% of the core zone (from the earlier 10%/15% in smaller parks and 20% in larger parks) (Pabla 2015).

Nobody has paid any attention to the provision that "Any core area in a tiger reserve from which relocation has been carried out, shall not be used for tourism infrastructure." If this provision is implemented, it will have the same effect as banning tiger tourism, as core areas of virtually all the important tiger reserves have been created by relocating villages. Thankfully, infrastructure for NTCA meant only residential accommodation, not the safari roads.

Similarly, another deadly provision which says that "Management of habitat to inflate animal abundance for tourism purposes shall not be practiced within the core or critical habitat" has gone unnoticed. Although the word "*inflate*" seems to have been used by mistake, the sentence seems to prohibit, shockingly, good wildlife management aimed at improving animal abundance in the tourism zones, which almost invariably means core zones.

Even NTCA is struggling to make up its mind on how the baseless 20% limit on tourism zone is to be implemented. At first, NTCA said that only a 20-meter belt on both sides of a tourism road shall be deemed to be part of the tourism zone. This would have allowed the use of virtually the entire core zone for tourism. Equally irrationally, it has now directed that every forest compartment (usually an area of 200–300 hectares) through which a tourism road passes, shall be considered a part of the tourism zone. As the existing tourism zones cannot be enlarged, even if they are smaller than 20%, any tourism in a new tiger reserve shall be a violation of the guidelines. Interestingly, this provision was retained in the guidelines despite the objections of some members of the committee who termed it "arbitrary".

The strange method for calculating the carrying capacity for safari vehicles is deliberately meant to keep the number of visitors to insignificantly low levels. If implemented scrupulously these levels can generate no benefits for the parks or the people. No wonder that most parks have found dubious ways of keeping their visitor intakes virtually at the levels at which they were operating when the new guidelines became effective. Perhaps, aware of the weaknesses of its prescriptions, NTCA is too embarrassed to ask any questions. Interestingly, the methodology for calculating the carrying capacity was never discussed in any of the committee meetings.

In fact, the guidelines suggest two separate approaches to determining sustainable tourism levels in tiger reserves, namely, the "Carrying Capacity" approach and the "Limits of Acceptable Change" approach, both given as annexures. However, nobody has paid any attention to the latter as the carrying capacity methodology has been circulating in the country since the days when Dr. Rajesh Gopal was the Field Director of Kanha Tiger Reserve, without anybody ever examining it critically. Strangely, although the guidelines themselves mention that the *carrying capacity framework has come up for criticism especially in the context of wildlife/nature based/ecotourism*", still the country is unable to think beyond these illogical numbers.

Impact of the Guidelines on Wildlife Tourism

Strangely, despite NTCA having such a strong stand against wildlife tourism, it does not collect any data from its reserves on tourism intakes to justify it. Therefore, it is difficult to say anything about the impact of the tourism guidelines on park visitation, at the national level. However, if the experience in Madhya Pradesh is any indication, wildlife tourism in the country plummeted sharply under the impact of NTCA's continuous advisories and guidelines. The figures below show the impact of these guidelines on visitor numbers and park revenues in the state of Madhya Pradesh, which owns 6 of the 50 tiger reserves of India.

Figure 1: Impact of NTCA Guidelines on visitor numbers in tiger reserves and other parks of Madhya Pradesh.

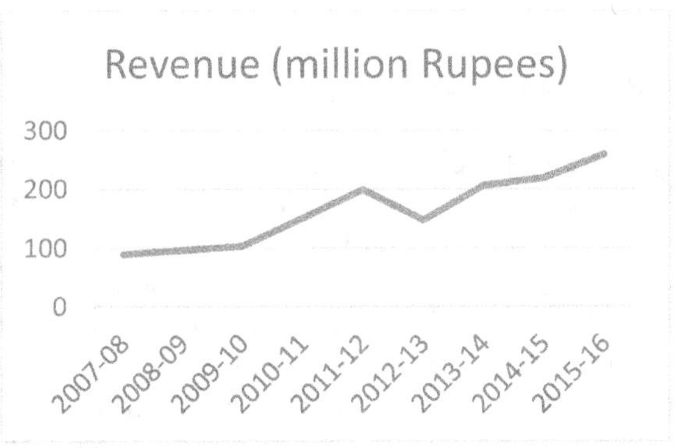

Figure 2: Impact of NTCA Guidelines on wildlife tourism revenues of Madhya Pradesh.

Although the state has 35 protected areas in all, five of the state's six tiger reserves receive most of the visitors. As can be seen, there was a stark fall in visits and government revenues as soon as the guidelines were implemented in the 2012-13 season. Although the revenue seems to be improving again, primarily due to increased tariffs, the number of visits to the state's parks has been stagnating around one million since 2012-13, while the previous trend showed a 10 - 15% annual growth. In fact, the number of foreigners in MP's parks has gone down by 50% in the five years since 2012 (Chundawat et al. 2017). It is important to note that all park revenues are spent on park management in Madhya Pradesh, and, this reduction in accruals must have made a serious impact on park management, especially in view of the falling GOI contributions in the last few years. Private businesses must have felt a similar impact, resulting in cuts in employment, primarily for tribal youth around parks, as well as along the travel routes.

Death of the Tiger Show

As the main objective of most of the visitors to India's national parks has always been to see a tiger in the wild, and the tiger is an elusive and cryptic animal, Madhya Pradesh Forest Department (MPFD) had developed a unique programme, popularly called the Tiger Show, to facilitate seeing wild tigers from elephant back. Until the early 1980s, a buffalo calf used to be offered as a bait to the tigers in the evening. The tiger would usually kill the bait in the night and would continue eating it for the next day or two. Experienced *mahouts* on elephant back would come looking for the tiger in the morning and would ferry visitors for a peep or a few pictures, if they found one. The tiger generally did not mind visitors coming on elephant back and would be completely relaxed, eating or sleeping, although there were some exciting moments, off and on. Cubs, if any, would continue to play and frolic around. The practice of tying a bait was stopped in the 1980s, on grounds of cruelty, but the tiger show went on. Now the *mahouts* would track random tigers very early in the morning, on the basis of field signs, such as pug marks, vocalisations, alarm calls etc. They would stay with it for some time until it was comfortable in their company and would ferry the visitors on elephant back to see the tiger, if the tiger was reasonably settled. As coming across tigers on safari drives was only a lucky chance, the tiger show almost guaranteed a tiger view and satisfied the lifetime desires of many. Thousands of people have seen their only wild tigers in this way. But when the NTCA guidelines provided that *"cordoning, luring or feeding of any wildlife shall be prohibited"*, it was interpreted as a hint to stop this practice. Although NTCA officials continued to say, privately, that the tiger show was not prohibited by the guidelines, they did not give it in writing. Thus, the tiger show is now dead. It is the loss of an opportunity to see wild tigers to thousands of people who are not lucky enough to come upon one on safari drives and the loss of a significant amount of revenue to the parks of Madhya Pradesh. Moreover, the security enjoyed by the tigers habituated to the presence of elephants and visitors, has been lost. It is common knowledge that tigers which are regularly tracked for tourism, lived longer and breed more successfully than others.

Although noises about the ethics of the tiger show, which involved some amount of manipulation of the tigers, had been made by purists earlier, the state continued with the practice as thousands of visitors benefited from it. Coming from the NTCA, despite their ambivalence about it, the practice has gone out of the window, though hopefully not forever. Although it was becoming more and more difficult to manage, due to high visitor interest in it, the Tiger Show (we had started calling it the *"sher darshan"* meaning, respectful glimpse of a tiger) was the unique selling point (USP) of Madhya Pradesh wildlife experience, which has now been lost.

Ideological Battles

In fact, the ideological battles between the state and the Centre had been raging long before wildlife tourism became a national issue in the wake of the

Supreme Court case. Our differences with NTCA on the management of tiger reserves were almost irreconcilable, as we were keen to pursue a rather pragmatic path while NTCA was insisting on a more hard line, exclusivist approach. We strongly felt that the autonomy and creativity of the states was being seriously stifled by the Centre, mainly NTCA, by issuing too many advisories and guidelines, without ever sharing the responsibility for inevitable failures in the field, as indicated by the Chief Minister in his letter reproduced above. In order to make the state fall in line, the NTCA started blaming every accident of man-wildlife conflict on, allegedly, wrong tourism practices followed by the state. Even if lightening had struck someone, NTCA would have blamed it on the wrong tourism policies of the state.

Once, when a *chara* cutter (a mahout's assistant) was killed by a tiger in Kanha, the NTCA member secretary wrote a stinging letter (dated 13/14.12.2007) to the CWLW, cleverly calling his directions as "suggestions for compliance" to show that he was now the boss. In an equally hard-hitting rebuttal of the insinuations, the CWLW, Dr. P.B. Gangopadhyay, summed up our approach to wildlife tourism. I hope the contents of the NTCA's letter are adequately reflected in the reply reproduced below.

"While I appreciate your concern on the subject and acknowledge your right to issue guidelines to any person or authority (whether that includes another statutory authority as well, needs to be established), in this particular case, your concern seems to be founded on some misunderstanding of the facts. Before I respond to your 'suggestions

for compliance' specifically, I would like to inform you that the recent cases of human deaths in Kanha had nothing to do with tourism as these happened in the Supkhar range which has always been out of bounds for tourists. The unfortunate death of the chara cutter is a freak incidence, as the same practice, of the chara cutters retrieving the feeding elephants from the forests early morning, has been in existence for more than fifty years, in all the tiger reserves of the state, without any incidence. Similarly, the cases of tigers hunting livestock close to Tala village is nothing new, although that has always been a matter of concern for us, too. But when the same particular tiger family killed and ate a woman some time ago, and we had decided to move the male cub out of the park, you intervened to advise otherwise. Similarly, the tiger shows, though much maligned by some purists, along with being a high point for tourists in these parks, have been a great help in our learning about the nature and behaviour of tigers. We do not accept the statement that these accidents have anything to do with the age-old tourism practices followed in Madhya Pradesh but recognize the fact that in situations where human beings and wildlife live cheek by jowl, accidents are likely to happen off and on. This is borne out by the fact that more human beings are killed and injured by wildlife outside the protected areas, than in the protected areas. The so-called habituation of tigers to human presence in the tourism areas, should, logically, make them more tolerant of human presence, not overly aggressive, as seems to be inferred by you. While we wholeheartedly agree that we should be conservative in developing tourism infrastructure in our protected areas, we also recongnise the fact that not only has tourism been primarily instrumental in raising public awareness about the need for the conservation of our wildlife and other natural resources, but it has also been a great direct help in protecting these resources. This is borne out by the fact that the presence of tourists deters criminals from entering well-visited areas, to some extent, and the tourists have also been acting as our extended ears and eyes by regularly reporting the presence or acts of criminals to the authorities.

However, we do admit that there is always scope for improvement, and we will continue to refine our park management practices. There is also no denying the fact that tourists and wildlife should be separated by a 'critical distance' and we scrupulously advise our park managers to ensure the same. As far as your 'suggestions for compliance' are concerned, our position regarding each one of them is as follows:

1. *We have already worked out and imposed tourist carrying capacities for our major destinations, along with online booking of entry passes. However, we had to modify and simplify the methodology, for the calculation of the carrying capacity, as we did not find the one circulated by you logical enough. The rotation factor, and some of the other assumptions, especially the correction factors, in the said methodology were too arbitrary and subjective to be defensible in the public domain.*

2. *We have no plans to develop any new tourism infrastructure in our protected areas and are sufficiently aware of the legal provisions. However, we do not intend to phase out our existing facilities as these are too small to be of any consequence and are located at our major administrative locations only.*

3. *We do try to maintain as much distance between the tigers/other animals and visitors as possible, as you know well. It is more than 30 meters in most cases.*

4. *As far as the question of opening new entry points to parks is concerned, we would like to leave that decision to the local authorities. If it helps in dispersing the existing tourist load from overburdened critical areas, and also strengthens protection of the new area, we would not like to prohibit such measures just as a matter of principle.*

5. *We agree, in general, that no new eateries or cafeterias should be created inside the parks, but minimal facilities, where visitors are required to spend time visiting interpretation centres or otherwise, should be seen as in order.*

6. *We agree that radio collared, injured or otherwise encumbered tigers should not be tracked for tourism purposes, but if such animals are tolerant enough and are easily visible, there should be no reason why they*

cannot be seen by visitors. We agree that they should not be bothered and detained just for the convenience of the tourists. In any case, the tourists prefer to see tigers which do not seem to have been doctored through radio collaring etc.

We would strongly advise against regulating tourist infrastructure in the non-forest areas, outside tiger reserves, by using section 38 (2) of the Act. This will create a huge antipathy towards conservation, as already there are fears of this provision having the potential of obstructing development in the rural areas. As you know, the process of declaring areas around protected areas as 'ecosensitive zones' is already under way and such developments should be regulated only under such general administrative provisions, through a consensus between all the relevant administrative agencies, rather than under the forest laws.

At the end, I would like to thank you for reminding us of the value of our tiger reserves and their differences from the large parks in other countries. I would like to assure you that we are acutely aware of the uniqueness of our protected areas, and if anything we have done or propose to do, has given you an impression that we have lost sight of these values, we would gladly review our position to ensure that such suspicions are suitably dispelled. At the same time, I would also request NTCA to kindly allow some space for outside wisdom and innovations as well, for the benefit of conservation." Unquote

Patrolling the Tiger Land

When the NTCA started sending advisories to the states to phase out tourism from the core zones of tiger reserves, many states were in the process of delineating buffer zones for the tiger reserves, which had become mandatory under the amended law. Tiger reserves like Periyar and Parambikulam in Kerala state had developed some fantastic, low impact, award-winning ecotourism products, involving trekking and camping, in their core areas, by then. In order to cope with the impact of the guidelines, Kerala converted the areas where these programmes were located into buffer areas. Strangely, some of these patches of buffer zone are now located at the heart of their core areas!

I had visited these parks and was very impressed with their popularity and value to the parks. Therefore, when I returned as the CWLW, after a few months in wilderness, in the wake of the Panna debacle in 2010, I tried to replicate the Kerala model of ecotourism in Madhya Pradesh and designed a programme titled "Patrolling the Tiger Land" under which the tourists could participate in a forest patrol, of course for a hefty fee. The idea was to allow visitors to appreciate the life of a forest guard, while adding some novelty to the lonely life of a forest guard, besides letting the visitors experience the wilderness closely. Our field officers were quite enthusiastic about it. However, as soon as the scheme was picked up by the media, NTCA sent advisories to all the states, that visitors should not be allowed to join the patrolling parties as poachers may pose as visitors and may access sensitive information. The Minister for Environment and Forests, who was otherwise a very objective person, wrote a personal letter to the Chief Minister of Madhya Pradesh to stop this scheme immediately. Although the state did not scrap the scheme and wrote back to GoI that it disagreed with them, we put the scheme in cold storage, in order to avoid another confrontation with the Centre. Forest walks are still allowed in our parks (reluctantly by some managers), but the scheme that would have transformed wildlife tourism in the state continues to be in suspended animation till today.

Unfortunately, Periyar suspended (perhaps resurrected under different names later) two of its most popular trekking programmes, the Tiger Trail and the Jungle Patrol, in the wake of this controversy, as they did not want to stand up to the NTCA. The hallmark of these programmes was that they were managed and led by former poachers and criminals. If Kerala could trust poachers for years, why we cannot trust caring citizens, to let them go into our forests, NTCA may explain, please.

The Truth about Tigers and Tourists

Incidentally, NTCA started tightening the screws on tourism at a time when India's tiger populations were recovering from an all-time low of nearly 1411 animals (year 2006). The tiger numbers grew to 1706 in 2010 and then to 2217 in 2014, mostly in heavily visited tiger reserves. Tourism volumes in tiger reserves also grew during this period, until they were cut down by the guidelines, as illustrated in the figures from Madhya Pradesh above. This obviously shows that there is no negative relationship between the growth of tourism and tiger numbers. Interestingly, most tigers, in tiger reserves, live within the tourism zones.

In the Pench Tiger Reserve of Madhya Pradesh, which had one of the fastest growing tourism volumes during this period and was also adjudged as the best-managed tiger reserve in the country in 2010, the tiger population increased from 17 to 24 in the core zone between 2006 and 2012 when the number of visitors increased from just 45,500 to 71,850 during the same period (Majumder et al. 2012), as shown below:

Table 1: Tourism and tigers in Pench Tiger Reserve

Year	No. of Tourists	Tiger Population
2006-07	45556	17
2007-08	54027	22
2008-09	62752	22
2009-10	52554	23
2010-11	65133	22
2011-12	71850	24

A more recent study in Ranthambhore shows a virtually linear relationship between the growth of tourism and tiger populations, as the visitor numbers grew from nearly 320,000 to 465,000, and tiger population from approx. 45 to 65, as shown in the graph below.

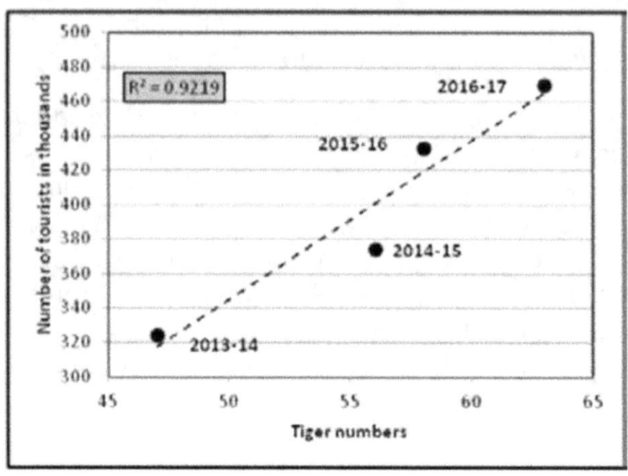

Figure 3: Relationship between increase in tiger number and growth in visitation. (Chundawat et al. 2018)

Majumder et al. (2012) found no significant difference between the tiger densities in the tourism zone and the rest of the core zone of Pench Tiger Reserve, although the measured densities in the tourism zone were higher than the rest of the park, i.e. 4.8 and 3.8 animals per 100 km², respectively. One famous tigress produced, astonishingly, 26 cubs, in 7 litters, and raised most of them successfully, in the tourism zone of Pench, between 2008 and 2017, showing that growing tourism had no adverse impact on tiger survival rates.

Cynics might say that the growth in tiger population in Pench and Ranthambhore was not *because of the* increase in tourism, but, even if they accept that it was *despite* the growth in tourism, the argument in favour of wildlife tourism is clinched!

But, despite clear indications that there was no negative relationship between tiger populations and tourism, NTCA continued its unrelenting attack on wildlife tourism until it was satisfied that it had dealt a deathblow through its infamous guidelines. Despite tourism being one of the most dominant activities in tiger reserves, NTCA still does not collect any information on tourism so that it can draw any conclusions. All its advisories and guidelines are based on either hearsay or personal prejudices of the officers that run the show.

Adversity leads to innovation

One positive impact of these guidelines, however, has been that tourism has now spread to the buffer zones of some tiger reserves, due to the restrictions on the number of safari vehicles entering the core zones. Some parks have also started allowing camping and night drives in the buffer zones. Although most of the buffer zone forests are degraded, and do not have much wildlife, they do have some good patches which offer some scope for recreational activities. In a ridiculous circular, however, NTCA is reported to have directed the parks not to improve the buffer habitat as it may lead to enhanced human-wildlife conflict, by attracting animals to the buffer zone. NTCA seems to be adept at tying itself in knots!

Furthermore, lodges have also been forced to look for some other cultural or archaeological attractions, outside the parks, to keep their guests busy when they cannot enter the parks for excursions. The reduction in traffic in the parks, as ordained by these guidelines, must have improved the quality of experience in the parks to some extent, but whether this improvement was worth the loss suffered in terms of park revenues and lost jobs will always remain an unanswered question. A far better way to improve visitor experience could have been to spread the traffic over larger areas, thinly, rather than reducing the intake. How many tribal kids had to drop out of schools because their parents lost jobs and how many more animals were poached because of lowered guard (due to shortage of funds) will never be known.

Despite the said guidelines announcing that ecotourism *"can help to contribute directly to the protection of wildlife or forest areas, while making the local community stakeholders and owners in the process"*, this entire saga reflects the mindsets ruling the Indian conservation scenario at present. Although NTCA was forced to admit in the Supreme Court that *"many people depend on tourism for their livelihood and ... stoppage of tourism may be a threat to wildlife and forests ... and common citizens would be deprived of an opportunity to appreciate our natural heritage"*, it is clear that these guidelines are not in sync with these admissions. The guidelines tend to limit the economic gains from wildlife tourism to an insignificant level, without any scope for growth in the future, they also tend to overload critical areas by confining the traffic to less than 20% of the total area. NTCA has also directed that no new entry points for tourists can be opened in the core areas of tiger reserves of Madhya Pradesh, which means all future infrastructure and commercial ventures, if any, have to come up near the existing entry points. This will concentrate its ill effects (garbage, overcrowding, pressure on forests for fuel wood, wear and tear of roads and other infrastructure, and so on) in the existing areas while preventing the spread of benefits of tourism (new jobs and incomes, appreciation of properties etc.) to more communities while they continue to bear the losses caused by wild animals. Neighbouring communities also have to suffer the restrictions imposed by conservation laws on activities like grazing livestock and collection of timber and non-timber forest produce etc., from the reserve's forests, which were their traditional ranging grounds.

Conclusion

Saving India's wildlife requires linking its presence with the welfare and prosperity of rural and tribal communities. Wildlife tourism is the only means of doing it, although it alone will not be enough. The tiger is perhaps the most gorgeous wild animal in the world and can be the backbone of the development of rural India in many states, if marketed and managed properly. With India's burgeoning middle class, growing global interest in wilderness and wildlife, and India's vast wild lands inside and outside tiger reserves, nature tourism is bound to grow. India will have to welcome and harness it to improve the lot of its teeming millions. However, if tigers and other wild animals just continue to contribute to India's poverty, and India does not learn to exploit their appeal for removing poverty soon, the animals shall be gone one day, but poverty shall remain! Although tourism is one of the five Ts (Technology, Tourism, Tradition, Trade and Talent) that constitute the Brand India of the NDA government, it remains to be seen whether NTCA will support this mission wholeheartedly or will continue to treat wildlife tourism as an imposition on tiger conservation.

Post Script

In our open democracy, where every document of the government is accessible to the public under the "Right to Information (RTI)" Act, NTCA is determined to keep its tourism guidelines beyond public scrutiny, even five years after they were issued. It seems, NTCA discovered, perhaps to its dismay, that WII was planning to "Review of the impact of the ... Guidelines on Tourism in Tiger Reserves" in a workshop, sponsored by NTCA itself, on "Ecotourism and Visitor-Use Management in Protected Areas" in August 2018. NTCA immediately forbade WII from going ahead with the proposed review, showing them the law, and asserting that NTCA "alone" had the mandate "to lay down the normative standards for tourism". God save the country if NTCA has to show the law {section 38 O (2): NTCA's powers to ensure compliance with its directions} to WII without whose support NTCA would have been just a lame duck!

CHAPTER 7

The Unfinished Dreams

Why unfinished

Bringing the tiger, gaur and blackbuck back to where we had lost them from, giving wildlife tourism the centre stage it deserves in wildlife management, and recognising the role of fire in keeping the grasslands healthy and productive were the most significant achievements of my seven year stint in the office of the Chief Wildlife Warden of MP, more than half of it as APCCF. As I was at the helm only for less than three years, that too in two tenures, a long list of my dream projects remained almost untouched when I retired in February 2012. These projects remained unimplemented because I needed permissions, some statutory and some administrative, and resources, for their implementation, which could not be garnered in time. Everyone knows governments are slow but how this sloth stifles and shackles creativity within the government is not well appreciated by the public. I remember my seniors advising me to be patient in my younger days, but somehow I could never really learn patience despite claiming to have a rather stoic attitude to life. When, despite pleading and cajoling, I heard nothing from the governments, both the state and central, for months, on projects pending with them for approval, I used to wonder why we have a structure in which even the heads of departments do not know what they can or can't do. Sometimes I used to joke with my colleagues that we would have transformed the state if we did not have the Vallabh Bhawan (secretariat) to slow and stop us. On most issues that matter, the head of department (HoD) requires the approval of the government which is advised by the secretaries who generally have no understanding of the subject. The secretary (these days principal secretary or additional chief secretary) himself needs to be advised by the HoD before he or she can advise the minister. Rarely is any real value added to a proposal which is not of a purely administrative nature in the secretariat, while it can be held up there for months and years, till the ministers, secretaries or the HoDs themselves get changed. On top of that, we have to deal with the bureaucracy in GoI and we have seen, in previous chapters, what GoI does to states' initiatives.

A very interesting, although extreme, example of how the governments cannot get going on matters which may have even the highest priority, is the case of allowing hunting of crop-raiding animals in MP. I had been advocating this idea, as a conservation measure, for several years when the forest minister in the then Congress government heard of it, sometime in the year 2002. Although I was not in the wildlife wing, he asked me to draft a proposal to allow hunting of wild pigs in croplands, to please the farming voters. The wildlife wing, which was headed by a rather conservative officer, was not happy, and instead implemented a watered-down version of my proposal on the subject, under pressure from the minister. When I moved into the wildlife wing in 2005, I picked up the thread once again and proposed a comprehensive system of sport hunting of pest species, with a provision that the returns would go to the affected communities. The BJP forest minister, who was also a Jain, liked the proposal but was bound by his religion which prohibited the killing of anything. So he directed his deputy, the minister of state, to approve the proposal. We prepared a précis for the cabinet but before it could be sent to the cabinet, both the minister and the principal secretary were changed. Before the proposal could move forward again, it was time for the elections in 2008, and the government did not want to take any risks with a potentially controversial move. After the elections, I was caught up in the Panna mess and could not pay attention to my pet idea for some time. Then I was transferred out of that office but returned within a year. By then there was a new forest minister who had become quite fond of this idea. He wanted to push it and got several revisions done to his satisfaction, but could not move forward because at least two successive principal secretaries stonewalled the idea on one count or the other. They were against the very idea of killing wild animals for any purpose. The minister was ready to overrule the secretaries, but, unfortunately, before he could do it, he happened to mention the idea to the chief minister in a review meeting of the department. The CM summarily dismissed the proposal. That was the last I heard of it until I retired in February 2012. The minister, despite his conviction, did not dare go back to the CM to convince him of the importance of the proposal to farmers' welfare and conservation of wildlife. Thus the proposal died after ten years of long incubation. In the meantime, six forest ministers and six principal secretaries had changed.

Although this was a controversial proposal which would have been rather difficult to accept, for any government, not all the proposals are so difficult to accept or reject. Still no decisions are taken on them for years, despite serious efforts by the protagonists. Given below is a brief description of the projects which could have changed the way conservation of wildlife is done in India but never saw the light of the day till I demitted office. Although not all of them are dead yet, it is unlikely they will be taken out of the closets for further examination any time soon.

Sport hunting of crop raiding species

Nilgai, wild boar and blackbuck are the most important mammalian crop pests in India. Although poaching of these species is rampant, the crop losses and the crop protection costs to the rural poor are still huge, running into billions of rupees. Farmers keep demanding a solution to the problem but the government does not do anything beyond cosmetics. Most states have made perfunctory rules to allow killing of nilgai and wild pig but nowhere have serious efforts been made to reduce their population in croplands, except perhaps the black buck translocation programme in Andhra Pradesh. Allowing people to solve their problems themselves by killing the animals illegally will exterminate the species one day while hiring hunters to reduce the population to a certain level will be very expensive and slow. People also deserve to be compensated for the losses incurred by them as the conservation laws do not allow them to solve their own problems. But crop compensation systems do not work satisfactorily in any state due to some inherent problems in the assessment of losses and, of course, corruption. I had been advocating a sport hunting system to reduce the populations of these species outside forests, and to generate funds for compensating losses, and tried to push these reforms during my tenure as the CWLW, but without success. We know sport hunting generates funds many times the meat value of the quarry. I wanted these funds to go directly to the affected communities who could do whatever they thought wise with these resources, after compensating the losses of the local farmers. But despite several successive ministers being strongly in favour of the idea, for almost 13 years, when I was a part of the senior brass of the department, the proposal did not go beyond the drawing board, except the ineffective boar hunting rules promulgated in 2004. Although most states have cosmetic rules for hunting of nilgai and wild pig, these rules are not effective anywhere. The primary reason for them to be ineffective is that the hunters are not allowed to use the trophy or the meat and they are obliged to hand over the carcass to the authorities for burning and burying. As bagging a single animal can cost the hunter tens of thousands of rupees in terms of time, fuel, labour, ammunition, permit fee etc. hunting it illegally makes better sense as the farmers are obviously happy not to report the offence. Translocation of these animals to forests, despite in-house expertise, is so expensive that MPFD seems to have abandoned this idea after just one successful effort in which some 27 *nilgais* were captured. Perhaps, one day, better sense will prevail and our political leaders and bureaucrats will have the courage to go the whole hog and implement the proposal to help conservation as well as communities.

Reintroduction of tigers in Madhav National Park

This tiny national park in the north of Madhya Pradesh had a resident population of tigers till the late sixties when Marshal Tito of the then Yugoslavia photographed four tigers on a kill. The Scindias of Gwalior had constructed a brand new lodge, the George Castle, to host the British monarch George V on a tiger hunting trip to the area in the nineteenth century, so famous was the place for tigers and tiger hunting.

But it had no tigers when I entered service in 1977, except some transients passing through it from Ranthambhore to Southern MP. Madhav national park was, in fact, a recreation ground of the Scindias, as they created facilities like a sailing club, shooting boxes, watch towers, a golf course, beautiful boat landings and *baradaries etc.* around a scenic manmade lake, in the middle of a vast wilderness of erstwhile Gwalior state. Although, perhaps, Scindias had never thought of using the place for preserving wildlife, beyond what was required to entertain their royal guests, a small national park was created in 1955. However, when the prime attraction of the area, the tiger, was lost, Scindias started dreaming of seeing tigers there again and started pushing the state to reintroduce the species. I remember a meeting of the state wildlife board in 1984, to which the late Madhav Rao Scindia was a special invitee, convened only to discuss his proposal for introducing tigers in the national park. As a result, a tiger safari, in a large enclosure, was created there in the nineties. The tiger population in the safari increased to about 8 or 9 when it was suddenly cut down by an attack of feline leucopenia. The only surviving tigress, Shivani, from this clan was later shifted to Bhopal where it died at a very ripe age. After the safari was closed, we had almost forgotten the tigers of Madhav national park.

As mentioned elsewhere, I started dreaming of introducing tigers there after seeing the documentary 'Living With Tigers', in which John Varty (JV) of South Africa successfully taught two captive born tiger cubs to be wild. Although we developed a much simpler process for rewilding captive tigers later on, at that time the method used by John Varty in the film appeared to be the only way to do it, as he taught the tigers all the tricks of the trade personally, like we teach our children. I thought we could contract out this job to someone like JV, who could introduce tigers in the park at his own cost, while making money from documentaries of the process. A committee constituted by the government to examine the scope for reintroducing tigers in Madhav found the park eminently suitable as it had plenty of prey base and recommended the introduction of two females and one male, all wild. Although it was not what I had dreamed of, still it was a lot for me. We sent the proposal to the NTCA/GoI for mandatory approval, which approved it with an impossible condition that a buffer zone should first be notified for the park. There was no way it could have been done as no state wants any more areas to be dedicated to conservation due to the difficulties faced by local people. We then had to put Madhav on the back burner as all hell broke loose in Panna about the same time and we got busy with rebuilding the Panna tiger population. The Panna experience of rewilding tigers reared in captivity gave me a new hope for Madhav, as we had five orphans waiting for rehabilitation in the wild. So, I rewrote the proposal to use these orphans to create a tiger population in Madhav and requested NTCA/GoI to waive the condition for creating a buffer zone and allow us to go ahead with the implementation. Despite clear agreement on the idea, expressed in several conversations, we never got the permission before I retired. I kept hearing that GoI was likely to give a go-ahead to the project after my retirement, but now the idea seems to be dead. The idea has been in the works for over twelve years now. With the evacuation of the last of the nine villages situated in the extended park, over 400 km^2 of pristine wilderness will remain a virtual conservation wasteland if tigers do not return there, either on their own, or through a reintroduction programme. Incidentally, around 2009-10, DNA analysis of scats found in the Shivpuri landscape indicated 6 tigers in the area but later on tiger signs completely disappeared. As the park is virtually starved of funds, since only tiger reserves get adequate funds in India, a reintroduction programme could do wonders for the area. A reintroduction programme would also help retain the tigers dispersing from Ranthambhore in this park, as the conditions will improve and the transient tigers will have an opportunity for securing mates.

I had started thinking that, perhaps, its time had already passed as I was not sure the state had the gumption to undertake a basically risky job, even if the GoI/NTCA approve it. But the introduction of tigers in Noradehi WLS this year, after 10 villages were relocated, has revived my hopes again.

Reintroduction of white tigers in Sanjay Tiger Reserve:

White tigers were found in the wild all over the tiger-bearing world, from India to Siberia, throughout history, but now we have none, although there are several hundred in captivity all over the world. "The Journal of The Bombay Natural History Society reported 17 white tigers shot between 1907 and 1933. E.P. Gee collected accounts of 35 white tigers from the wild up to 1959, with still more uncounted from Assam. ... Victor H. Cahalane reported white tigers in northern China in 1943: ... These tigers were white individuals of the Amur tiger subspecies (*Panthera tigris* altaica), also known as the Siberian tiger. White tigers were reported in northern China and Korea. White tigers have cultural significance in both countries. They are also part of the folklore on Sumatra and Java" (Wikipedia).

White tigers were found all over India as shown in the map:

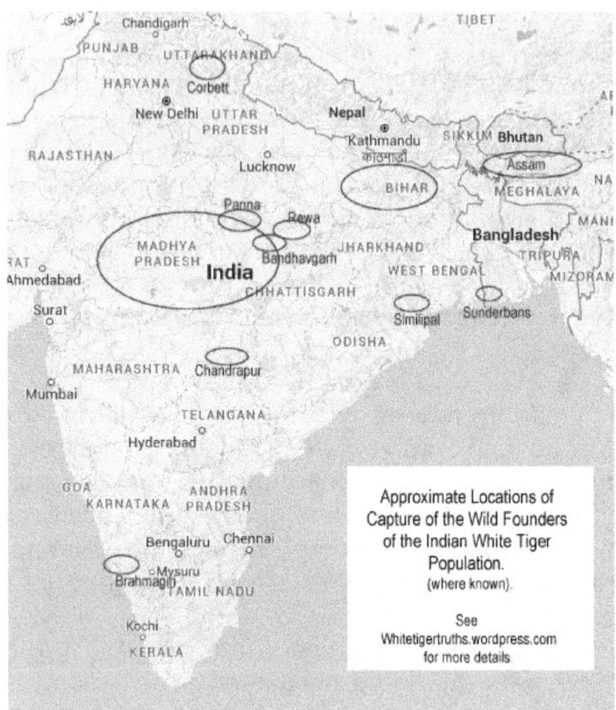

Figure 4: Locations of captured white tigers (https://whitetigertruths.wordpress.com/)

The Maharaja of Rewa captured the last wild white tiger in 1951 from the forests of Sidhi district, now part of the Sanjay Dubri Tiger Reserve, although there are reports that another white animal was shot in 1958 (Sankhala 1997). This tiger, Mohan, is the founder of virtually the entire white tiger population in the world.

About the time we had successfully rewilded tigresses reared in captivity, in Panna, I heard of a project to conserve white lions in Africa in the wild. So, I too started toying with the idea of reintroducing white tigers back to the wild, in its native Sanjay Tiger Reserve. I am surprised that nobody had ever thought of this as it should be an obvious thing to do. If we can use the tiger as an icon in whose name we are trying to save the Indian wilderness, the flagship value of the white variant should be even more. When I broached the idea to friends, they scoffed at it, mainly on the count that 'it has no conservation value', or 'why preserve a recessive gene?' 'they will not survive in the wild', etc. I completely failed to understand these arguments. Conservation is all about preserving the diversity of nature and the white tiger is a very conspicuous element of this diversity. Sanjay tiger reserve had virtually no tigers back then, although it is reported to have a few now, and, consequently, had the lowest priority in the allocation of funds among all tiger reserves. I thought if we could start a project to reintroduce white tigers in this park, it will immediately become a prominent park and would attract all the resources it required for effective conservation, including for shifting the 50-odd villages. The Central government rejected the project saying, on the advice of WII, saying that "the white tiger does not represent a unique lineage of tigers but is an aberration caused by recessive alleles and therefore are not of significance to merit conservation efforts of reintroduction". By that time I had retired and nobody contested this decision of GoI. Only recently I learnt that the GoI rejection was, in fact, engineered by my own office after my retirement. I knew this project could not happen during my life in service, but I developed the project just to set the ball rolling in the hope that it might catch somebody's fancy someday.

Although there are NGOs demanding the extinction of white tigers and the global associations of zoos have banned the breeding of white tigers in zoos for some dubious reason, the Exotic Genome Repository (EGR) which is "a collaborative effort bringing together scientists from multiple academic institutions, conservationists, veterinarians, and animal husbandry specialists in an effort to direct scientific resources towards preserving these vulnerable species for future generations," (http://exoticgenome.org/index.php), clinches the issue with the following statement on their Facebook page: *"There is a mountain of misinformation being spread about white tigers. They are not defective. They are not unhealthy. White is conferred by a single base mutation in a single gene. We should STRIVE to keep the genetic variant of white coat color present in the captive population. If anyone tells you different, send them here and we will set them straight!"*

(https://www.facebook.com/ConservationThroughGenomics/ photos/rpp.1577600195843441/1578981495705311/?ty pe=3&theater).

Although the original project idea was more complex, involving setting up an in situ conservation breeding facility to produce pedigree white cubs for rewilding, relocation of several villages, fencing of a 100 sq km area, and translocation of ungulates from elsewhere to bolster prey availability, things have become much simpler over time. Many of these steps have already been taken or are under way, independent of this proposal. A white tiger safari has been created at Mukundpur, near Rewa which can easily be used to produce white tigers of desirable genealogy, if need be. Several villages have already been relocated, creating a beautiful habitat for tigers and prey. More villages are being translocated. Nearly 500 spotted deer have already been translocated from Bandhavgarh, and more is planned. A few tigers have also been translocated here from other parks, which have done well without fencing. There also seems no need to train the founding animals in jungle craft before release, as we initially thought necessary, as several parks in MP now have successful tigers which were raised in captivity, and were released in the wild without any pre-release conditioning or training to hunt in the wild. Thus the only thing that needs to be done is to release one or more tigers with a white gene into the wild, while strengthening protection on the ground and continuing the village relocation and prey induction programmes. The founder stock must be sufficiently outbred pure Royal Bengal animals so that they do not carry any deleterious genes, acquired during their inbreeding history, into the wild. Over time, we would have a tiger population with a sprinkling of white gene, and some animals will be of white colour as well. Although the project is not going to be as expensive now as I initially thought, it will still require considerable funding which can easily be generated by carefully marketing the filming rights of the project. John Varty, who also has white tigers at his private tiger reserve in South Africa, is already prepared to bid "millions of dollars" for exclusive filming rights if ever such a project is undertaken.

Although GoI has rejected the proposal, however, WII scientists agreed "to examine its merits, feasibility, and subsequent best strategy to reintroduce the white tiger gene in a wild tiger population" when I shared the historical records of white tigers in Indian forests and their "value" to Indian natural heritage.

Incidentally, I have raised this issue in every meeting of the state wildlife board, without generating much enthusiasm in the department. However, some debate over the issue has started in the media and let us hope real science and conservation consciousness will win in the end. The project seems to be dead at the moment, but who ever thought we would have tigers, gaurs, *barasingha*s and blackbucks back after local extinctions? All these projects were rejected, or suspended in the middle, before they created history! Just imagine what Sanjay Dubri Tiger Reserve can do to the development of the area if it becomes the only place on earth to see white tigers in the wild.

Reintroduction of lion and cheetah in Kuno Sanctuary

It has been more than 20 years since the GoI decided that the lions of Gir will be given a second home in Kuno wildlife sanctuary. Gujarat has stonewalled the move under a mistaken notion that they would lose their monopoly over the species. Gujarat is not ready to reduce its intransigence over the issue despite the Supreme Court's order (April 2013) to provide a founder stock for a new population in Kuno. However, realizing that we are unlikely to be able to get the founder stock from Gujarat in the near future, the GoI directed Madhya

Pradesh to examine the option of using zoo-born Asiatic lions to start the Kuno population in 2007. We promptly submitted an action plan for breeding lions for introduction in Kuno but never heard from them again, despite the fact that the Central Zoo Authority had given us RS. 43 lakh for building the lion housing facilities. When prompted to take a decision from time to time, the proposal was found missing from GoI cupboards and the state was asked to submit a fresh proposal. By that time we had learnt something about wilding captive cats, through the Panna experience, and submitted an updated proposal to them again in 2011. However, by that time the pure bred zoo lions, selected for conservation breeding in 2007, in various zoos, had either died or had become too old for breeding. But before the matters could be decided, the PIL took the matters out of the hands of the government and everybody was waiting for the conclusion of the court proceedings before making the next move. As the Gujarat Government is unrelenting in its opposition to the project (because Narendra Modi has committed in the state assembly that he would not give even a hair of the lion for this project), and there is no progress even five years after the order of the Supreme Court (which has issued contempt notices to the parties), MPFD has recently proposed to the GoI that they would like to go ahead with the zoo-born animals. Whether the Kuno population is created by translocating a founder stock form Gir, or through conservation breeding, it is a project which will catapult India into the frontlines of conservation in the world as, so far, we are seen by the world community only as a passive country which does not see conservation beyond anti-poaching. Let's hope better sense will prevail after the death of 23 lions in Gir due to canine distemper in September 2018 and the acceptance of a contempt petition against the parties.

Although the Supreme Court opened the door to the second home of the lion, the same court blocked an equally important conservation initiative aimed at reintroducing the cheetah in India, nearly 60 years after its last record in the country. The court first imposed a stay on the reintroduction of the cheetah in Kuno, in May 2012 and forbade it completely in April 2013, allowing the lion project to go through. Although GoI is pursuing the matter in the court, the matters are at a standstill at present. The grounds on which the project has been blocked are weak and fallacious and would, hopefully, be rejected whenever a proper discussion is held in the court.

I felt hugely excited when GoI selected Kuno for immediate reintroduction of the long-lost cheetah in the country in 2010. Although the matter became controversial from the very beginning, for me it was nothing short of a miracle happening in front of my eyes, as things do not happen so quickly in India, ever. The lion reintroduction project had been coming for twenty years, without being anywhere near the horizon, while the cheetah project was ready to take off within a few months of its announcement. While the people pushing the project were saying that they wanted to rejuvenate the grassland ecosystems in the name of the cheetah, on the same lines as the forest ecosystems were being protected in the name of the tiger, the anti-cheetah lobbies were arguing that the cheetah project would usurp the scarce resources meant for tiger conservation, and that the arrival of the cheetah would block the way for bringing the lions to Kuno. As Kuno is an important staging point for tigers transiting from Ranthambhore towards Madhya Pradesh, there was also the question of keeping this link intact. Vested interests also disowned the cheetah as a part of Indian heritage. They also said that our cheetah was different from the African variant being introduced. Lay people naturally wanted to know whether lions, cheetahs, tigers and leopards, all big cats, can live together or not. Although all these questions were convincingly addressed by the protagonists of the project, the wind went out of the sails of the project with the exit of the minister, Mr. Jairam Ramesh, from the ministry of environment and forests. The final blow came when Gujarat cunningly argued in the Supreme Court that Kuno no longer needed lions as the GoI and MP had decided to introduce cheetahs there. The court issued an injunction that the cheetah project would be stayed till the fate of the lion case is decided by the court.

For me, none of the scientific and emotional arguments in favour or against the cheetah project carried much weight, as some of these were essentially biased. My support for the project was based on the sole reason that the arrival of an iconic species would bring some economic development to an impoverished region, in the form of tourism, while reversing the extinction of an important piece of our heritage. Moreover, it would raise the profile of the Indian conservation community significantly. I was, naturally, in a hurry because of my looming retirement. The cheetah taskforce was also keen to do it quickly because they could not be sure of the same level of proactive support after I was gone. Kuno was absolutely ready to receive the cheetahs as all the 24 villages had already been shifted in the name of the lion project and there was plenty of prey base. Only some fences were to be repaired for housing the cheetahs for acclimatisation and observation for a few months, and the winter of 2011-12 was set for the transfer of the cheetahs, to be donated by the Cheetah Conservation Fund, Namibia. But the exit of the minister and the court injunction halted everyone in their tracks. Perhaps, someday, better sense will prevail, as I have said in several other places, and Kuno will become the only place on earth where seven free ranging large predators, namely tigers, lions, cheetahs, leopards, wolves, hyenas and wild dogs, will create jobs for local people through tourism. Of course, the grassland ecosystems will be recognized as productive lands, rather than wastelands, helping species like the lesser florican and the great Indian bustard to return, and India will have the most well-known extinction of its wildlife, that has happened in living memory, reversed. Although it is not important which cheetah breed is introduced, hopefully it will be the Asiatic one as the ongoing efforts to produce the variant, from the stem cells of the last remaining individual in Iran, may be successful by the time the decks are cleared here.

Reintroduction of barasingha in Bori Sanctuary

This dream of mine has already become a reality. Wow, wow!

The sub-species of *barasingha* (swamp deer) found in Kanha national park is called the hard ground *barasingha* (Cervus duvauceli branderi) because it does not need swamps to survive, unlike the true swamp deer of Dudwa and Kaziranga. Kanha has been able to recover the only surviving population of the sub-species from a low of only 68 animals, in the seventies, to the current level of approximately 700 animals, spread over all parts of the park. A few animals have been seen even in the Phen Sanctuary, which is nearly 30-40 kilometres north of the national park. Although the Kanha population is now doing well, a single population of a species is never enough to protect it against total extinction due to causes beyond human control. Therefore, the department has long been trying to create new populations of this species, both inside and outside Kanha. In 1982, nearly 20 animals were lost in the process of translocation to Bandhavgarh and the project was abandoned for good. As a compromise, the park management has gradually built a second population, translocating one or two animals at a time, in the southern parts of the park, some 30 km away from the nearest natural herds. A large number of animals were lost even in this short distance translocation due to capture-related complications, and the department had abandoned all thoughts of further tinkering with the population until recently. When we experienced great success in translocating 50 gaurs from Kanha to Bandhavgarh in 2011 and 2012, I started dreaming of creating another *barasingha* population somewhere as an insurance against its possible extinction in the Kanha landscape. High levels of predation being one of the factors inhibiting the growth of the species in Kanha, I ruled out Bandhavgarh because of high tiger density there. I had been eyeing the Satpura landscape as a possible new home for *barasingha* for some time as Captain James Forsyth had seen *barasingha* in this area on his way to Pachmarhi in 1862, but it did not have the large grasslands required by the species for foraging. But as soon as the Dhain and Bori villages were shifted, the idea started haunting me, as the village sites got transformed into ideal *barasingha* habitat. We promptly developed a project proposal to translocate 20 animals to a 25 ha enclosure in Bori sanctuary. The herd was to be allowed to grow to about 50 animals, before releasing them in the wild, while retaining a few animals in the enclosure, safe from predation. More villages were in line for relocation and Satpura complex seemed to have all the ingredients of supporting a viable *barasingha* population, more so because it did not have a high predator density. Govt. of India surprised us with the speed in issuing the permission for translocation, perhaps impressed with our record in gaur translocation. We got our South African friends on board and set about creating the infrastructure for the job. A 27 hectare predator-proof boma was created in Bori, and capture options for the animals were evaluated, under the supervision of Les Carlisle, who had spearheaded our gaur translocation project. The dates for the operation were set in February 2012, after the *barasingha* rut was over. But when we lost half the animals in the ill-fated translocation of blackbuck to Kanha in November 2011, GoI promptly cancelled the *barasingha* permission and asked us to submit a Population and Habitat Viability Analysis (PHVA) report on the new habitat. The said analysis was promptly conducted by the State Forest Research Institute (SFRI) in collaboration with WII, and we submitted the report to GoI in February 2012 itself. The analysis endorsed our decision and found the new habitat even better than Kanha, capable of supporting a viable population of nearly 500 animals. The PHVA recommended a viable founder population of 100 animals, instead of 50. However, the GoI permission for the translocation did not come for three years. Fortunately, under persistent pressure from the state, translocation of *barasinghas*, to build up a viable founder population in an enclosure before release into the wild, began in the month of January 2015. The translocated animals are already breeding in their new home and the population reached 60, including more than 20 local births, by the end of 2017. They are expected to be released into the wild in 2018 or 2019, after the induction of a few more animals from Kanha and some more local births.

Interestingly, the permission to translocate barasinghas to Satpura was given by GoI only after the state proved its capacity to do it by translocation of 7 barasinghas to Van Vihar Bhopal. Successful translocation of barasinghas to Satpura Tiger Reserve has restored the reputation of MPFD as a competent translocation agency, after it was seriously dented due to the death of several blackbucks within two months after translocation to Kanha. In view of the reluctance of GoI to give a go ahead for the project for years together, most of us believed that it would never happen as there was no dreamer behind the project. However, my successors proved the naysayers wrong by forcing the hand of GoI by their sheer persistence and rare self-confidence in undertaking a potentially risky endeavour.

The lucky barasingha is one of the several endangered species, such as the Asiatic lion, the hangul or the Kashmir stag (*Cervus canadensis hanglu*) which need a second home as a measure of insurance against a possible extinction due to man-made or natural disasters. While GoI should have been leading this renaissance in wildlife conservation, it continued to stifle the state's initiative for years, just because the mandarins were afraid of having to share the blame in case of a possible miscarriage of the operation.

Reintroduction of horses for patrolling

Horses should have been natural companions for foresters but somehow we parted ways long ago. A forester has to go off-road for patrolling and inspections and horses can easily make it more convenient and efficient. When I started feeling that the reason why we are unable to check poaching may be because our staff was patrolling only motorable roads, and at best footpaths, which poachers can easily avoid, I started thinking of ways to make off-roading a viable patrolling option. One reason why forest subordinates are unable to comb their areas frequently is that we have loaded them with so many responsibilities that even a forest guard has only a few days in a month to patrol his forest. In an empirical assessment of the commitments of a typical forest guard, I was stunned to realize that 26 days in a month he is committed to do jobs other than patrolling his beat. A DFO had an impossible 41 days' commitments in a month. As a result, their visits to the forests are always hurried and rushed, rather than searching for criminals behind bushes and boulders. With the aging of the department, as a result of erratic recruitments over three decades, forest patrolling became even more superficial by the 1990s and continued to decline till recently. Induction of the new forest guards, after the year 2000, did not seem to improve the situation as the new recruits just do not want to stay in the forests and had their bikes to go back to the towns after a quick inspection of their beats. They all have working wives and children going to English medium schools. Horses came to my mind as an option to remedy the situation, as sermons and orders had no effect. I thought horses would make the cross-country patrols, and inspections, much more convenient, efficient and attractive. Horses would also add some glamour to the forest service, and, perhaps, officers would try harder to get away from their offices to enjoy a horse-back inspection.

So, when I was convinced of the value of horses to a forester's profession, I started discussing the idea with the field staff on my tours. Most of them were very enthusiastic. Some of them said that they used to maintain horses in their younger days but had to sell them as government did not give any support for their maintenance. However, one thought bothered them all: how will the horses deal with the tigers and leopards? Some had earlier used horses in areas where predator densities were not high, but now they were going to patrol the tiger reserves. Moreover, the horses were then used mainly for point to point travels, between destinations, rather than for scanning and scouting the forests for poachers. So I sent a few questions across to South Africa, where horses are quite regular in conservation work. This is how Jeffery Cooke responded:

"The idea of using horses to increase patrol effectiveness has been used by EKZNW for many years and there are currently 3 sections in Hluhluwe Imfolozi Park that maintain horse units. In terms of the predator situation the horses become very used to the dangers in the park and are always very alert to possible danger. There have been very few confrontations on patrol and only one fatality which occurred in the mid 80's. ... I personally believe that horses play an invaluable role in patrol effectiveness and would not hesitate to implement this initiative."

This was in June 2009. As this was a new direction for the department, I requested the government to give me an in-principle approval of the idea before spending more time and energy in fleshing it further. But I lost my job as CWLW, though temporarily, in August 2009 and the matter went into cold storage. On my return next year, I started thinking about the issue again and had discussions with local mounted police on the implications of having a horse unit and sent further questions on the subject to South Africa. Jeff Cooke's response was as follows:

"The horses are usually structured around a ranger outpost and they are used by multiple riders (whoever is on duty). The horses are stabled in the reserve and are attended to by a dedicated groom who is responsible for feeding and general care and maintenance. The resident section ranger is responsible for overseeing the animals and usually keeps the records of each horse with vaccination history and a summary of the number of hours it has been used on patrol. Of importance is the selection of the right types of animals and here we look for "salted stock", i.e. from the same or similar area. We go for hardy bush types rather than thoroughbred stock. We then put them through extensive training using our most experienced riders and paired with experienced horses."

So, the die was cast, although I did not have time on my side to push for a decision, due to my looming retirement. I proposed a small pilot unit in one of the parks but never got any response from the government, despite everybody praising the idea in conversations. I believe my successors are not keen on the issue, as despite my dropping hints off and on, no one has picked up the thread so far. Interestingly, Sahyadri Tiger Reserve in Maharashtra has started experimenting with horses (mules), perhaps triggered by a chance conversation I had with the Field Director, Ben Clement, in 2015. Although I am excited about this initiative I am also worried that if it is not done correctly, and fails, it may seal the fate of the idea for long. If only wishes were horses!

Public private partnership (PPP) in ecotourism

I was not particularly aware of the potential of ecotourism as a conservation and development tool until, quite fortuitously, the then PCCF, the late Mr. DP Singh, in 1998, directed me to develop a concept paper on developing ecotourism outside protected areas. As the internet was not much help those days, I racked my head for a few days and submitted a brief outline, "for PCCF's eyes only", of a concept I called "Recreation Forests". He liked it but we made no progress with it before he retired. However, a few days of thinking about the subject convinced me that selling natural beauty is a much more sustainable forest management strategy than just producing timber and bamboo. Since then my thoughts on the subject have been evolving, as more and more literature became available on the internet. Ever since I started thinking about ecotourism, I have been more and more convinced that we will not be able to exploit its potential unless the private sector comes forward, not only for selling but also for the development of the ecotourism product. Since then, I have been advocating the PPP mode of developing ecotourism in the state, because the state neither has the technical and financial resources nor the marketing capability to attract sufficient volumes of visitors, while the private sector has all these strengths aplenty. However, private investors can be expected to invest their money only in ventures where they have a reasonable assurance of earning a profit without their competitors taking benefit of their investments, i.e. they would like to have an exclusive access to a forest area which they would develop as an ecotourism destination. The latest form of this evolving concept is something like this:

- The Forest Department shall divide the Government forests into Ecotourism Blocks of approximately 50-150 sq km each (or whatever size is found suitable) and shall appoint private operators as ecotourism agents through a suitable competitive process, in consultation with the concerned communities. Only the agent, so appointed, shall be entitled to issue ecotourism permits to visitors in his block.

- The operator (agent) shall have no right over the land or forest produce, including sequestered carbon, of the area.
- The government shall have no obligation to change the management of the forest areas concerned and the normal forestry operations, as per the prevailing working plan, shall continue. Future working plans, however, may have ecotourism as one of the objectives of management of the said forest.
- The local people shall continue to use the forest area as permitted under the law and prevailing regulations. However, the agent shall be free to come to an agreement with the local people to change their forest use practices by paying compensation for moderating or discontinuing activities such as grazing livestock or collecting fuel wood etc.
- The use of the area shall be allowed only on a 'take nothing away and leave nothing behind' basis.
- The agent shall be allowed to use the reserved block only for giving his clients (visitors) an exposure to nature and natural processes through nature walks, trekking/hiking, bird watching, camping, game drives, watching wildlife etc.
- The agent shall not be allowed to do any construction in the forest area except preparing temporary camping sites, temporary/portable toilets, hides/machaans etc. required for experiencing nature, which require no clearing or breaking up of the forest land.

- No cutting of trees, for any purpose, shall be allowed. However, light clearance of ground vegetation for the purpose of demarcating nature trails etc. can be allowed.
- The agent shall be obliged to employ local youth in all operations, as far as possible. Lodging of tourists with local home stay facilities shall be encouraged.
- The revenue received from the venture shall be shared with the local communities as per government policy of Joint Forest Management.
- The agreement with the agent shall be for a period above ten years so that he has an incentive in developing the forest as an attractive ecotourism destination and a reasonable opportunity to recover his costs. However, there can be a provision for a mid-term review.
- The agent shall have no claim over the use of existing buildings and other infrastructure of the forest department in the area. However, he may be allowed to use this infrastructure on payment of a fee as may be determined by the department from time to time.
- Public servants on duty shall have unhindered access to the area but they shall not interfere with the operations in any way.
- All operations shall be subject to prevailing pollution, conservation and other laws applicable for the time being.
- In order to protect the operator from petty harassments from lower officials, the

power to impose penalties, if any agreed in the agreement, shall be given only to senior officers of the department.

- The agreement may be cancelled only with the prior permission of the government or the PCCF.

Almost 20 years of my advocacy of this concept has not moved it forward an inch. State government and my colleagues in the department have been primarily wary of the Forest (Conservation) Act, 1980 (FCA) despite the fact that the FCA does not come in the way. The FCA says that "any work relating or ancillary to conservation, development and management of forests and wildlife" even if it requires the "breaking up or clearing of any forest land" does not amount to the use of the forest land for a "non-forest purpose" requiring the prior permission of the GoI. Thus, the question to be addressed, in evaluating an ecotourism project, is whether it aims to improve the "conservation, development and management of forests and wildlife" or not, which, obviously, a project on the above lines would do eminently. The misconceptions about the FCA are so deep-rooted that, until I had gone so deep into the matter, even I was of the same opinion. Although FCA has been a very powerful tool in saving India's forests, its misuse to prevent forest-friendly activities is clearly counterproductive for conservation.

Although ecotourism, in the form of wildlife tourism, is the public face of the forestry sector, GoI considers ecotourism as an anti-forestry activity and is unlikely to change its opinion any time soon, and PPP in ecotourism is going to remain a mirage. We did receive a proposal on the above lines but the GoMP asked the investor to get a sense of GoI's opinion on the issue before considering the proposal. The protagonist, Julian Mathew of ToFTigers fame, made a presentation to the GoI mandarins, in a clearly hostile environment. At the end of the meeting, the Director General of Forests (DGF) insultingly asked: "How many retired forest officers are you offering jobs to in this project?" That was the end of the discussion on the subject in Delhi.

However, taking a pragmatic view on the issue, PCCF MP, at the instance of the MP Ecotourism Development Board, where I was an adviser for some time after my retirement, issued a circular in October 2012 that private businesses and communities may be allowed to become 'vendors' for selling ecotourism permits in government forests, and thus create businesses providing logistics and hospitality services to the visitors, without any exclusive rights on any forests. This is a good move, as private operators, alone or in partnership with local communities, may use this facility to develop nature resorts near scenic forests. As private businesses will explore potential destinations only gradually, the pioneers in the field are likely to have a virtually exclusive access to the nearby forests for quite some time, before competition discovers *their* forests. However, the operator will not be interested in investing in improving the condition of the forests and wildlife, which he would have done had he had an exclusive right to this forest. But something is better than nothing, and, perhaps, one day we may also see PPP operators investing their capital and negotiating with local communities on ways of improving government forests to make them more attractive to visitors.

With the advent of Forest Rights Act 2006 (FRA), and large forest areas going under community control, perhaps some communities would like to try their hand at this idea. As civil society orgainsations (CSOs) are so keen to kick FD out of the forests, this may be one tool to show to the world that communities can do what the government could not dare for years. (Please read the next section also.)

Hiring private lands for conservation

We all know that our PAs are relatively small and there is not much scope for their enlargement in view of the reluctance of the states to put any more public lands, and people, at the mercy of our conservation laws. However, there are private agricultural or fallow lands adjoining the PAs which can be added to the PAs by compensating the owners suitably. The cost of cultivating these lands is very high as they are ravaged by wild animals. In many cases such lands are just left fallow by the owners. However, these lands are quite tempting for the tourism industry and will, sooner or later, end up as lodge properties. A good wildlife lodge can be a much more wildlife-friendly land use than agriculture, especially if there is no fence between the lodge and the PA, but we have few such lodges in our country. Thus either the existing local owners of these lands are condemned to eke a difficult living out of them or they can sell it to the lodge builders. If the farmer continues to farm it, he may also be tempted to use live wires, snares and traps to protect his crops. So, we proposed to the government that we take these lands on rent from the farmers on a medium term lease. Under the agreement, the farmer would leave the land fallow for use by wild animals in exchange for an annuity which will be equivalent to or better than his net income from the land. Thus, while the PA would expand de facto, the farmer will earn more from his land, and will not be tempted to sell his land to the lodges. However, the proposal was rejected by the government, though after my retirement, without any discussion. Despite this setback, I am hopeful that someday wisdom will prevail and we will be able to expand our PAs beyond their existing boundaries by purchasing or hiring adjoining crop lands, as there is virtually no other option. In fact some donors were ready to support this line of action, and were already negotiating deals regarding some critical pieces of private land wedging into some PAs in MP for transfer to the PA management.

In a path-breaking move, Maharashtra has already gone ahead and issued "Guidelines regarding establishing Community Nature Conservancy" (dated 21st October 2015), in which the state has invited owners of farmlands in the neighbourhood of PAs to convert their lands into wildlife habitats and set up ecotourism businesses, either individually or as cooperatives. Even private corporations can set up such businesses. The highlight is that the land owner shall be compensated for any losses he incurs by dropping agriculture in favour of wildlife conservation. Thus the state is promoting wildlife conservation along with ecotourism, including PPP, which is an ideal combination. While MP has been dithering on the idea for decades, a progressive state has moved forward. Although they have allowed the use of adjoining forests for ecotourism, which is great, Maharashtra can perhaps move one more step to reach an ideal situation, by giving exclusive access to the conservancy to some part of the adjoining forests so that the conservancy can invest in the improvement of habitat and wildlife densities on it. Kudos, Maharashtra!

Rehabilitation of nomadic hunting communities in non-hunting livelihoods

It is well known that most tribal communities living in remote areas hunt wildlife for food and small-time trade/barter. But there are some communities, tribal as well as non-tribal, who travel far and wide in search of game and do much more damage to ecology than the settled hunting communities (such as *baigas, bhils, bharias, madias* etc.). The most well-known nomadic hunting community is called *pardhi* although not all *pardhis* go by that surname.

The word *pardh*, in Hindi and several other associated languages, also called *akhand shikaar*, means a day of communal hunting when every member of a certain community goes hunting wildlife, generally on an auspicious festival day, such as Holi. Although the practice is well-known only in a few regions such as Bastar in Chhattisgarh and Simlipal in Orissa, it is probably prevalent in most traditional communities that have evolved in the wilder parts of the country as mentioned by Verrier Elwin (2002, reprint) in his treatise on the Baiga tribe. The *pardhi*, i.e. the hunter community with several sub-divisions based on hunting specialisations, and sub-castes, such as cheetah *pardhi*s, bail-*pardhi*s, Rajput *Pardhi*, Faase *Pardhi*, Gaaye *Pardhi*, Bhil *Pardhi*, Raj *Pardhi*, Langot *Pardhi*, Harar *Pardhi*, Paal *Pardhi*, Dhangar *Pardhi*, Ghod *Pardhi*, Ghisaadi *Pardhi*, Maang *Pardhi*, ShikaJ *Pardhi*, Lamaan *Pardhi*, Chiche *Pardhi*, etc. (http://*pardhi*samaj.blogspot.in/) is an ancient nomadic hunting community whose entire culture and way of life revolves around the hunting of wild animals and birds. Perhaps there are hundreds of hunting communities, known by different names, in different states, specialising in hunting/trapping different species and using different techniques. These people live in small, scanty, makeshift huts and roam the countryside in search of good hunting opportunities. They are so skilled and deadly in their art that no animal can escape their determined bid to bag it. These skills and several kinds of their nets, traps, snares etc. have evolved over hundreds of generations of practicing this vocation. They can be commonly seen camping along the forest boundaries, in small tenements of 1–5 hutments covered with polythene sheets, scouting the forest for game, ranging from quail, partridges, wild boar, deer, antelope, right up to tigers and leopards. The blame for clearing the forests from wild game, in most areas, can largely be placed on their shoulders. Although traditionally they were hunting for their own food and some small sales and barters, the boom in international trade in wildlife products has propelled some members of the community into big-time smuggling rackets. Most of the tiger and leopard skins and bones, and several other species, circulating in the international market generally owe their origin to the deeds of these communities. These people used to be employed by the erstwhile rulers for assisting them in their big game hunts and for training their hunting animals (cheetah *pardhi*s), and are still employed by local farmers for protecting their crops against the depredations of wild animals. They kill wild animals, such as wild pig and blackbuck, while protecting the crop fields, and share their booty with their employers in exchange for protection against legal action.

Apart from the *pardhi*s, some other communities such as *bawarias, bahelias, chirimars* etc. are also deadly nomadic hunters. *Bawarias* are concentrated mainly in north India while *Pardhi*s are in central and South India.

Interestingly, many members of the infamous Sansar Chand gang belonged to the *pardhi* and *bawaria* communities.

With the depletion of game due to habitat loss and overhunting, and the consequent ban on all kinds of hunting, their craft, culture and lifestyle became illegal and they became criminals without any crime, in true sense. With the decline in game availability even for illegal hunting, some of them entered other criminal activities such as thievery, thuggery etc. but a majority have stuck to their traditions, fully or partly. They were notified as a criminal tribe by the British and are popularly (ignominiously) known as a denotified criminal tribe today. Many of them, both men and women, have started small roving businesses, such as trading in cheap cosmetics and undergarments, junk, essences, etc. but are generally believed to be using these businesses for scouting the area for criminal opportunities. They can also be seen selling fake *shilajeet, kasturi* (musk) and many kinds of bogus cures for incurable diseases. People begging in the name of Shani god, small children begging at city crossings and teenaged girls carrying infants in their arms, soliciting alms, are often from a *pardhi* background. They hardly get any opportunities as wage labourers as most people detest them as lazy and unreliable. Their children hardly ever stay in schools due to the discrimination and humiliation faced by them from other castes. They are unable to access any benevolent government programmes, as much due to the lack of awareness of such opportunities as their varied social classification.

Traditional hunting communities are found in every state although their concentration in central India, especially Madhya Pradesh, Maharashtra, Rajasthan etc. is better known. They are generally believed to be tribals, but are classified differently (Scheduled tribes, scheduled castes, OBCs, general) in different places, even within a state.

Whatever their official classification, they carry the stigma of being a criminal community wherever they go. As a result, they have had virtually no opportunities for changing their traditional lifestyle and continue to do inestimable damage to the wildlife and ecology of not only MP, but most other states as well. Stray efforts to give them a settled life, through grants of agricultural land, have generally failed, as, either they never got possession of the land in question, or the quality of the land was so poor that it did not interest them. Even if they have become cultivators, here and there, they continue to practice their traditional profession of hunting as a side job. A similar situation prevails in almost every state.

An estimate of the total population of the hunting communities in the whole country is not easily available, as they are known by different names in different states. One website (https://joshuaproject.net/people_groups/17847/IN) mentions the population of just one such community, the *pardhi*s, to be 286,000 in the country. Another site (http://www.peoplegroups.org/Explore/GroupDetails.aspx?peid=41619) mentions the *pardhi* population in Marathi—Konkani region to be 182,000. Another study gives the Madhya Pradesh population to be 20,000 families, although almost every village (over 50,000 villages in MP) has a few households of *pardhi*s. Wikipedia mentions that a sub-division of *pardhi*s, the phans *pardhi*s, number 60,000 in Mumbai alone (These may no longer be wildlife hunters). Going by these indicators, the population of all such communities (i.e. nomadic hunters) may not be less than a million in the country.

I have long held the view that as long as this community continues with its way of life, conservation of wildlife will be very difficult, in view of the perfection of their art and their nomadic culture. If nothing else, they would certainly trap partridges and quails for food and some cash. Taking an imaginary example to illustrate the deadliness of their profession, a single *pardhi* family would need 365×8=2920 partridges, or equivalent numbers of other game, just to earn a bare minimum income of Rs. 200 per day, presuming that one partridge can get them approximately Rs. 25. Even if we presume that only 10,000 families are hunting full time, the total annual take can be as enormous as 29,200,000 birds or an equivalent number of other game!

So far, society has dealt with their criminal activities through policing and ostracism, but it has led us nowhere. They are of significant interest to police, as *pardhi*s, and some other communities (e.g. Kanjars), are the first target of police investigation in any theft case anywhere. But the forest department has never taken an interest in them except for keeping a wary eye on them whenever they set up camp around forests. Perhaps no forest department, except MP in a very small way, has ever thought of engaging with them as a part of their anti-poaching strategy. So far, the interventions to help them change their ways have originated out of the general mandate of the state for the upliftment of the lower sections of the society. These attempts have failed, at least partly, perhaps because the concerned development agencies had no commitment to their welfare beyond meeting the annual departmental targets. However, the failure of these agencies to make a difference to the lives of the *pardhi*s has resulted in continued loss of wildlife, which the forest department has the mandate to protect. Therefore, it is important that alternative approaches for dealing with these communities are tried by the conservation agencies and NGOs.

With this background, we urged our park managers to explore the possibility of engaging with these communities as a long-term solution to the depletion of wildlife. Although the forest department had gained some experience in working with rural communities in general, most officers were hesitant in working with criminal communities. However, G. Krishnamurthy, the field director of Panna Tiger Reserve, showed extraordinary capacity to deliver on this front and soon had a school for pardhi children, and a small unit employing about a dozen pardhis in manufacturing fencing posts, up and running. Although the fencing post production unit wound up after some time as it became financially unviable, due to lack of proper management, the school, operated in partnership with the Sarv Shiksha Abhiyan (Campaign for Education for All) programme of the government, survived for many years and is perhaps still running in some form. In fact, the education programme expanded from one school to two (the second one exclusively for girls). WWF India joined this effort after some time and is perhaps instrumental in sustaining this effort now, as the park management seems to be reluctant to remain intimately involved in this programme due to various difficulties. Another Mumbai-based organisation called The Last Wilderness Foundation (LWF) is also actively working with them. One reason why the park management started dragging its feet over this issue was that some sections blamed the Pardhi School for the decimation of the remaining tigers of Panna during 2008-09 period. They surmised, though without any evidence, that the parents of the children studying in the schools tried to remain close to their children and kept themselves busy in clearing the park of tigers. Later park managers, although they said they believed in engaging with the pardhi community, wanted such initiatives to be located away from high risk areas, particularly tiger reserves. Incidentally, some kids have also gone to college with the support of The Last Wilderness foundation.

Another school, this one for the children of the *movie* community, was started by the Madhav

National Park in Shivpuri district. These children were of diverse ages, as the schools functioned as "bridge schools" preparing them for regular schools, their grade depending upon the proficiency gained by them. I interacted with the children in these schools a few times and it was a fantastic experience. Like all children, they had dreams of careers as teachers, doctors and engineers. Some wanted to be forest rangers and even park directors. Many of them had seen their parents killing tigers and other animals, and had no hesitation in describing the chilling details. It was obvious that if they had not been in schools, they would certainly have been assisting their parents in poaching wildlife somewhere, even at that age.

The Pardhi population is quite thick in the Ganj Basoda tehsil in Vidisha district. I visited some pardhi camps in this area with the help of a local friend, Anil Yadav, who was trusted by pardhis and was able to see their lives a bit more closely. The camps had only women and children as the men had gone to the forest on *business*. I was permitted to go inside the tent which was absolutely bereft of any possessions. When I found no food inside, they informed me that they would eat only when the men returned, which may be later that day or the next day! I saw several kinds of traps, nets and snares used by them for catching different species. During a few visits I learned that although they were happy with the way they were living they were quite ready to adopt any other viable livelihoods. However, they were quite sceptic about my capacity to do anything for them as nothing had ever come out of any government moves to help them. Despite their scepticism, I convinced the MP Scheduled Castes Financial Development Corporation to provide assistance to them for self-employment. The corporation generously provided self-employment assistance, ranging from a few thousands to a few lakhs, to nearly 100 families. They surrendered their poaching nets and snares to the forest department in a function attended by ministers. Although it is difficult to hazard a guess as to how many have stopped poaching wildlife as a result of this initiative, I remember seeing press reports that crop damage had increased significantly since the pardhis had stopped hunting black buck and wild boar. The friend who introduced me to the pardhis does believe that many of them had in fact stopped poaching. This group continued to be in touch with me till my retirement and even came to bid me farewell on the day of my leaving the department. At least one of them still plies the taxi he purchased with the money provided by this programme and his wife is now a *sarpanch* of his village. This is quite a journey for a pariah community. WWF also tried to support our efforts in this area in the form of a school on the lines of the Panna school, but, perhaps, did not get very far.

WWF also started an initiative in Harda district to train pardhi ladies to produce handicrafts, based on their traditional skills of net making and knitting, but this initiative also did not progress well as WWF could not sell the products.

One organisation, called the Dalit Sangh, has been working with pardhis in Sohagpur (Hoshangabad district) for many years. I once had a short meeting with a few of these people. Only 6–7 ladies and one boy turned up for the meeting. I asked one of the ladies why her husband had not come for the meeting. She said he died while laying a live wire for killing animals. Quite shocked, I asked whether she had any children. She said her son also died a similar death. They all said that they kill nothing but partridges but most of the catch was snatched by policemen and other sundry officials. I asked the only boy in the group what would make him stop poaching wild animals. His reply was simple: *aap to hamare kandhe par haath rakh do, hum sab chhod denge.* What he meant was that he only needs protection against harassment and extortion. He said they were living a miserable life. They get no employment and if there is a crime anywhere in the area, the police rounds up pardhis before doing anything else. Whatever they get from the forest (e.g. partridges) is extorted by the police. He said the forest department had never paid any attention to them.

I tried to encourage the Dalit Sangh and the local forest department to work together for this common objective, but was not successful. They distrusted each other and the forest department was worried that it would be difficult to deal with pardhis strictly, in case of a crime, if they were also running welfare programmes for them.

I also tried to create an ecotourism programme in which pardhi youth would demonstrate their skills in tracking wild animals and their knowledge of the ethnobotany, but could not get anywhere. I had a few meetings with the pardhis of Nasipur village, inside Ratapani sanctuary, to guage their interest in ecotourism based on their traditional skills. My cajoling and tempting did not interest them much. On my request, Forsyth Lodge in Madhai willingly took two pardhi boys for hospitality training, in preparation for setting up an ecotourism venture for them. However, nothing came out of this move as well, as I left the country for a consulting job outside, while Forsyth Lodge was sold to new owners. Incidentally, LWF is still trying to set up a pardhi-centric ecotourism programme in Panna district and I desperately hope that it works out.

Although these initiatives were significant in principle, they were totally insignificant in scale. Although weaning even one professional poacher may mean saving hundreds, even thousands, of animals and birds over his life time, we need a pan-India programme to make a significant difference, looking at their country-wide spread and reach. Although most of the economic alternatives for them will have to be completely unrelated to their traditional vocations, strengthening their bonds with their culture, albeit in a controlled and refined environment, can also be considered if possible somewhere. Involving them in ecotourism as guides and naturalists can be absolutely thrilling as no other guides can compare with them in the knowledge and understanding of natural history. Allowing them sustainable hunting of some species seems to be a far cry under the current legal regime, but if we can allow sustainable harvesting of swift nests in Andaman and Nicobars, by the local people, such thoughts may not be completely misplaced.

Interestingly, I read in the newspaper yesterday that Panna Tiger Reserve is going to try pardhi guides trained by The Last Wilderness for tourism. WWF India and GTI Council have also shown interest in the idea of an all-India pardhi upliftment programme off and on, but nothing has come out of these conversations so far. Perhaps, someday, someone, somewhere, will pick up these threads and take these small beginnings to a level where their impact is visible and appreciable!

Bibliography

1. Chundawat R.S, V. Upamanyu Raju, Hemant Rajora and Julian Matthews, 2018. The vValue of Wildlife Tourism around Ranthambhore Tiger Reserve in Rajasthan on Wildlife Conservation and Local Communities. TOFTigers © TOFTigers & BAAVAN
2. Chundawat, R .S. 2008: *Nothing is Gained by Denial.* Sanctuary Asia, June 2008.
3. Chundawat, R. S, Merten, J. Agasti, S. Sharma, K. Raju U. and Matthews, J. 2017. Value of wildlife tourism for conservation and communities: a study around four tiger reserves in Madhya Pradesh (Part-I, Tourism infrastructure and revenue). Bagh Aap Aur VAN (BAAVAN) and TOFTigers.
4. Chundawat, Raghunandan Singh, Pradeep Malik and Neel Gogate: *Ecology of tiger: to enable a realistic projection of the requirements needed to maintain a demographically viable population in India.* Final Report (final draft). Study Period- 1996-1999. Wildlife Institute of India.
5. Chundawat, Raghunandan Singh, Pradeep Malik and Neel Gogate: *Ecology of tiger: to enable a realistic projection of the requirements needed to maintain a demographically viable population in India.* Final Report (final draft). Study Period- 1996-1999. Wildlife Institute of India.

6.   Dutta, J.J. H. S. Panwar, Ravi Singh, P.R. Sinha, Abhilash Khandekar, and RS Negi, 2010: *Lessons from Panna: Report of the Expert Committee on the Decimation of Tigers in the Panna Tiger Reserve. Report of the Expert Committee on Disappearance of Tigers from Panna Tiger Reserve.* Forest Department, Government of Madhya Pradesh, India.

7.   Elwin, Verrier (1939): The Baiga. Gyan Publishing House, New Delhi (Reprint 2002).

8.   Forsyth J. Captain (1871): Highlands of Central India, Natraj Publishers, Dehra Dun (Reprint 1994).

9.   Guidelines for the notification of Critical Wildlife Habitats. F.NO. 1-23/2014 WL. Government of India, MoEFCC. New Delhi.

10. Guidelines regarding establishing Community Nature Conservancy. Government of Maharashtra Revenue and Forest Department Government Circular No.: WLP 0315/ CR 56/F-1 Mantralaya Mumbai - 400032   Date: 21 October, 2015.

11. Iverson, S.J. (1982). *Breeding White Tigers. Zoogoer* 11: 5–12.

12. Jhala Y.V, R.Gopal, Q. Qureshi (eds.) (2008). *Status of the Tigers, Co-predators, and Prey in India.* National Tiger Conservation Authority, Govt. of India, New Delhi, and Wildlife Institute of India, Dehradun

13. Karanth K. Ullas, Raghunandan Singh Chundawat, James D. Nichol and N Samba Kumar, 2004: *Estimation of tiger densities in the tropical dry forests of Panna, Central India, using photographic capture–recapture sampling.* Animal Conservation (2004) 7, 285–290.The Zoological Society of London.

14. National Tiger Conservation Authority 2012: *Comprehensive Guidelines for tiger conservation and tourism as provided under*

section 38 O (1) (c) of the Wild Life (Protection) Act, 1972, PART-B: GUIDELINES FOR TOURISM IN AND AROUND TIGER RESERVES. Circular dated 15 October, 2012.

15. Pabla H. S. 1997: *Conflict Around Protected Areas.* - Vacham, NCHSE. April 1997. Bhopal, India.

16. Pabla H. S. 2008: *Nothing is Lost in Panna .... So Far.* Sanctuary Asia, June 2008.

17. Pabla H.S. 2015: Wildlife Conservation in India - 1: Road To Nowhere.

18. Pabla, H.S. 1984: *Panna National Park: Problems and Prospects. (Office report).*

19. Packer C. et al. (undated) Conserving dangerous animals: The lion, the fence and the way forward)

20. Packer C., A. Loveridge, S. Canney, T. Caro, S.T. Garnett, M. Pfeifer, K.K. Zander, A. Swanson, D. MacNulty, G. Balme, H. Bauer, C.M. Begg, K.S. Begg, S. Bhalla, C. Bissett, T. Bodasing, H. Brink, A. Burger, A.C. Burton, B. Clegg, S. Dell, A. Delsink, T. Dickerson, S.M. Dloniak, D. Druce, L. Frank, P. Funston, N. Gichohi, R. Groom, C. Hanekom, B. Heath, L. Hunter, H.H. Delongh, C.J. Joubert, S.M. Kasiki, B. Kissui, W. Knocker, B. Leathem, P.A. Lindsey, S.D. Maclennan, J.W. McNutt, S.M. Miller, S. Naylor, P. Nel, C. Ng'weno, K. Nicholls, J.O. Ogutu, E. Okot-Omoya, B.D. Patterson, A. Plumptre, J. Salerno, K. Skinner, R. Slotow, E.A. Sogbohossou, K.J. Stratford, C. Winterbach, H. Winterbach and S. Polasky : *Conserving large carnivores: dollars and fence.* Ecology Letters, (2013) doi: 10.1111/ele.12091.© 2013 Blackwell Publishing Ltd/CNRS

21. Ranjitsinh M.K. 2017. A Life with Wildlife. From Princely India to Tthe Present. Harper Collins India. New Delhi.

22. Sen, P. K. and Ravi Singh, 2008: *Report on Panna Tiger Reserve* to NTCA.

23. Sen, P.K., Qamar Qureshi, Chaturbhuj Behera and S.P. Yadav, 2009: *Report on Disappearance of Tigers from Panna Tiger Reserve.* Special Investigation Team, NTCA, New Delhi.

24. Supreme Court of India, order dated 12.08.2013 in IA 2202, 2203 in WP 202/1995 (TN Godavarman VS. UoI.)

25. Wildlife Institute of India, 2009. *Status of tiger and its prey species in Panna Tiger Reserve, Madhya Pradesh.* Final Report submitted to Madhya Pradesh Forest Department, Bhopal. Wildlife Institute of India, Dehra Dun. pp 36

About the Author

Harbhajan Singh Pabla grew up in a Punjabi village in India. He joined the Indian Forest Service in 1977 and retired as the Chief Wildlife Warden of the state of Madhya Pradesh in 2012. Apart from doing the usual things that an Indian forester does, he nurtured his love for the wild while managing national parks like Kanha, Panna and Bandhavgarh. Along the way, he developed a penchant for challenging the stereotypes that have ruled the conservation mindset in the country so far. He was responsible for changing the face of wildlife tourism in Madhya Pradesh, despite opposition from NTCA, and made tourism revenue a significant resource in the tiger reserves of the state. When Panna lost all its tigers, he developed and implemented the tiger reintroduction plan that has given the world the confidence that wild tigers will always be around.

He introduced a culture of active wildlife management in the country through the reintroduction of locally extinct gaur, blackbuck and barasingha, besides the tiger, in the extirpated habitats. Thousands of animals have been moved between Indian parks since then, on the strength of learning from his initiatives. Despite his retirement from IFS, he still dreams of seeing the white tiger back in the wild and his wish list also includes seeing Indian foresters riding horses for patrolling and enjoying the wilderness.

He was once on the faculty of the Wildlife Institute of India and is an international consultant in forestry and wildlife management in South Asia now.

He lives in Bhopal, India and can be contacted at:
E-mail: pablahsifs@gmail.com
Cell: +91-9425007850.

9 781795 878876